T

About the Book and Author

Examining recent European experience with industrial policy, Dr. Udis explores ways to ease the transition to reduced or redirected levels of military spending. He surveys government policies in Great Britain, France, West Germany, Sweden, Belgium, the Netherlands, and Italy, identifying strategies for individuals, firms, and regions as they adjust to shifts in the economy. Regional development, science and technology, and labor market policies are analyzed in conjunction with public procurement strategies and government aid for exports and international ventures. The book includes material drawn from the author's interviews with government officials and industry leaders, illustrating practitioners' perspectives on these measures and on the nature of diversification and conversion. Their views and experience, the author argues, will be valuable tools for policymakers weighing the costs and benefits of implementing industrial policies in the United States.

Bernard Udis is professor of economics, University of Colorado. He has published numerous journal articles and is the author of *From Guns to Butter: Technology Organizations and Reduced Military Spending in Western Europe* (1978).

The Challenge to European Industrial Policy

Impacts of Redirected Military Spending

Bernard Udis

Westview Press / Boulder and London

Westview Special Studies in International Economics

Copyright © 1987 by Westview Press, Inc.

Published in 1987 in the United States of America by Westview Press, Inc.; Frederick A. Praeger, Publisher; 5500 Central Avenue, Boulder, Colorado 80301

Library of Congress Cataloging-in-Publication Data
Udis, Bernard.
   The challenge to European industrial policy.
   (Westview special studies in international economics)
   Includes index.
   1. Industry and state—Europe. I. Title.
II. Series.
HD3616.E8U35 1987   338.94   86-19110
ISBN 0-8133-7234-8

Composition for this book originated with conversion of the author's computer tapes or word-processor disks.
This book was produced without formal editing by the publisher.

Printed and bound in the United States of America

⊚   The paper used in this publication meets the requirements of the American National Standard for Permanence of Paper for Printed Library Materials Z39.48-1984.

6   5   4   3   2   1

Contents

Tables and Figures

Acknowledgments

This study would not have been possible without the cooperation of many individuals both here and abroad, and I am deeply indebted to them. Unfortunately, the requirement of confidentiality forbids my naming them individually. However, I wish to express my profound appreciation to all those European executives, government officials, and scholars who gave so generously of their time to openly discuss sensitive matters. Their cooperation was critical to the success of this venture. In addition, I wish to thank the foreign service officers and other staff members of American embassies in the countries studied for their unfailing generosity and assistance.

There are several individuals whom I feel free to name and am obliged to thank for their help and personal involvement. John Lynch of the Office of Economic Adjustment of the U.S. Department of Defense provided me the opportunity to conduct the study out of which this book grew. Mrs. Sally Hofmockel prepared the seemingly endless versions of the manuscript with good humor and a high level of competence. Her new daughter, Amy E. Hofmockel, also displayed thoughtful consideration by delaying her arrival until her mother had completed the final manuscript. Susan McEachern of Westview Press cheerfully guided author and manuscript safely through the shoals of the publication process. Finally, I wish to express my deep gratitude to Margaret Grace Williams, who was, in a unique way, present at the creation of this work and supported it through every stage of its development.

Bernard Udis

1

Introduction

The goal of this effort is to extend an earlier study of European policy instruments available to ease the adjustment to reduced levels of military spending.[1] That study found few relevant European examples of mechanisms to aid effectively the transition of military productive capacity to civilian output. The updating effort was conducted during January 1985 in France, the Federal Republic of Germany, Sweden and the United Kingdom, supplemented by mail and telephone communications with sources in Belgium, Holland, and Italy.

All countries studied have an array of existing policies which might be helpful in easing a transition to lower levels of military spending, which collectively might be described as industrial policies.[2] Such policies typically fall into two categories:[3] micro-policies designed to help firms in depressed traditional industries and their dependent workers and communities, and specific policies whose purpose is to aid promising new industries (usually based on advanced technology) in gaining a foothold in the market. What these policies have in common is their going beyond the "macroimpersonality" of traditional monetary and fiscal policy. They include regional development programs, labor market programs, financial aid to firms at below market rates of interest, subsidies for research and technology, export promotion and financing, aid to innovation, etc. They will be described in some detail in the individual country sections. To give the reader a sample of the variety of such policies across the countries studied, a series of summary tables (Tables 1.1–1.7) appears at the end of this section tracing their evolution from the pre-1974 period through the reactions to the first series of oil price shocks of 1973–1974 and most recently through the changes of 1979–1980. Despite their diversity, they are linked by the fact that they were not designed specifically to aid a military to civil transfer of resources. Their origins are, of course, less important than their possible effectiveness in easing the strain of economic conversion. For this reason, the question of their potential relevance and usefulness in dealing with the economic conversion issue was repeatedly asked of government officials, industrialists, and other informed persons. Their responses appear throughout this volume.

Widespread concern over the economic and social strains which might result from a substantial reduction in the level of military expenditures was not encountered in any of the countries studied. The principal reason for this relative complacency is that military expenditures are seen as being a normal part of the government budget and likely to remain that way. While military expenditures represent a relatively small share of the gross national product, they do show some cycling over time, reflecting changes in geopolitical conditions and the more prosaic completion of large procurement projects with gradually lengthening periods of slack in between.

The typical government position is that cycles in military markets are sufficiently familiar to permit most firms to plan in advance for adjustment and the development of alternative products and markets. In other words, preparation for and adjustment to variations in military procurement is viewed as a normal managerial responsibility in a dynamic economy. This pattern is probably made more explicit in the Federal Republic of Germany than in most other countries, but the position is not unique. The Swedish government has demonstrated more interest in the general issue of economic conversion, as evidenced by several government studies and reports, but even there, few explicit policy actions can be identified.

A distinction must be made between government positions and the concerns of minority political parties and private groups. There is no shortage of concerns about easing the adjustment process among certain trade union groups, "peace" groups, and out-of-power political groups. It should be noted however, that while questions in the West German Parliament concerning the utilization of defense industry production capacity in the event of disarmament agreements often are raised by individual Social Democratic legislators, the official position of the current Christian Democratic government is almost indistinguishable from that of the predecessor Social Democratic administration; namely, that the responsibility of planning to meet such transitions is principally that of industry.

The logical question one would wish to ask is which policy measure "works" and which does not. Unfortunately, the answer is more complex than that. There is not an exact formula for successful economic conversion. Similar measures in the different countries do not yield similar results. This should not be surprising since every country's economic history contains a record of firms in the same industry and at the same point in time with widely differing profitability. Conversion or transfer of resources from military to civilian use is an example of adjustment to changing market pressures. Since the challenge to firms in this situation is to "adapt or die," one may reason that national environments which encourage such adaptation will enjoy higher success rates. The society's views and attitudes to adaptability and change may be as important as specific policy measures in explaining differential success.

In this context, the view of a French banker was particularly interesting. He expressed concern that the French economy's adaptability to change would remain low as long as French society continues to draw its leaders essentially from two institutions of higher education: the Ecole Nationale d'Administration and the Ecole Polytechnique. While acknowledging them to be excellent educational institutions, he saw them as stifling new ideas with their oppressive application of the old school tie or "old boy's network," thereby effectively locking the door to the "self-made man" type of executive who might be more inclined to consider less traditional approaches to problem solving.

The importance of flexibility applies to workers as well as to managers. European workers have long been noted as tradition-bound and resistant to geographical mobility. Sweden's active labor market policy appears to deal with these issues directly. An impressive program to subsidize geographic mobility exists there.

Regional development programs exist in each country, but they all face a common dilemma: the existence of depressed areas attesting to their loss or lack of attractiveness to industry. Efforts to develop new industry or to encourage the expansion of existing industry in such regions require measures to counteract this perception of industrial unattractiveness. In an ideally operating economy, both labor and capital would be freely mobile, responding to the drive for economic gain. The self selectivity of emigrants is well-known, leaving depressed communities populated by older, less educated, and more risk-averse people. Such persons are often less attractive to potential employers. The new technology-based industries are viewed as more mobile than more traditional industries which required proximity to raw materials and markets. Thus, high technology industries are often characterized as "foot-loose" and substantial competition occurs among communities to attract them. However, such firms have tended to concentrate in areas with easy access to research-oriented universities and laboratories, and highly-skilled workers. Evidence of the success of regional policies is scarce, as it is difficult to create locational advantages where they do not exist. Social and political realities, however, together with occasional market failure, have prevented governments from relying completely on a market-dominated industrial location process.

Individual country programs are diverse in their details and in their underlying philosophies. They vary substantially in their views of the appropriateness of governmental intervention. France is probably at the more-active-role-for-government end of the continuum, with a well-developed set of industrial policies. However, all countries accept the idea of strategic industries which are crucial to national independence and well-being. Thus, an official of the Swedish Industrifonden commented that the formation of his organization in 1979 in part reflected a concern over the effects on important firms of declining expenditures for military research and development and nuclear energy. Setting up the fund was "another way for the government to support large projects." Saab's civil aircraft work with Fairchild Industries of the United States,[4] and Volvo Flygmotor's civil aeroengine projects with Garrett, General Electric, and Pratt and Whitney, also of the United States, received substantial financial aid from the Industrifonden.

Also of importance is the government attitude toward the export of military equipment. In two cases, Sweden and the Federal Republic of

Germany, substantial government-imposed inhibitions to the export of military equipment exist, essentially ruling out expanded military exports as an adjustment path.[5] In the others, increased emphasis on exports is a predictable policy. Multinational collaborative ventures which expand the market and bring scale economies will also become more attractive.

It should be noted that in most of the countries studied, as in the United States, military production typically occurs in firms which also produce civilian products. Indeed, in some cases such as electronic components and vehicles, what makes a product "military" is the nature and identity of the buyer. Obviously, the adjustment problem will be more severe when there is a dependence on military customers and few alternative uses of the product. Similarly, the problem will be more severe if the workers, equipment, and plants engaged in military production are more specialized and harder to transfer to other uses. This suggests the importance of studying these particular issues as part of a strategy designed to ease transitional problems. Where military products are produced by nonspecialized military producers, such products are often seen as "fillers" to occupy company resources during slack periods of civil product sales. Among military producers, export sales often play a similar role.

Sweden's policy of armed neutrality has placed it in an interesting position related to reduced military outlays. Its major military project today is the production of a successor aircraft to the Viggen. The successor, designated Gripen, will be produced with about a fourth to a third of its parts coming from abroad. This arrangement insulates domestic industry, to some extent, from the full impact of reduced procurement. This tactic is obviously not available to all countries. Even in the case of Sweden, other factors were responsible for this outcome.

These strategies (to order military equipment from abroad or export military equipment) to ease the strain of reduced domestic military expenditures illustrate the importance of the context in which reduced military expenditures might occur. Thus, a widespread movement toward disarmament at the international level would mean a greater challenge to policymakers attempting to minimize the economic dislocations, since under these circumstances the export market for arms would be reduced. Having made this point which logic demands, one should hasten to counter it with two others. First, in a world characterized by resource scarcity, the freeing of resources previously devoted to military purposes opens the possibility of alternative utilization. While some might worry about how smoothly such a transition could be effected, it should be recalled that during 1945–1946 in what Boulding has called the "Great Disarmament," military expenditures declined about 30% in the United States with little unemployment and a large increase in both personal consumption expenditures and gross private domestic investment. Civilian government expenditures at all levels and net exports also grew.[6] Thus, if the goal of defense expenditures is national security and not job creation, misplaced fear of job loss should not become the rationale for military outlays no longer necessary on political and military grounds. At the other end of the spectrum, we must also note that the East-West confrontation is not the sole cause of conflict in the world, and the market for arms is unlikely to disappear following a hypothetical East-West detente.

Pursuing this line of reasoning, one should note that specific US-Soviet agreements to limit or reduce nuclear weapons are not synonymous with reduced military expenditures. If such agreements are reached primarily because the parties agree that nuclear weapons have lost a significant part of their political or military value but the persisting distrust of the other party's goals and motivations remains, existing political commitments will have to be met and larger conventional military forces may have to be substituted for the lower level of nuclear forces.[7]

Much of the remainder of this volume identifies and evaluates public policies available to aid the transition by producers of military equipment to reduced or redirected military spending. At the level of the firm many of these policies encourage industrial diversification and the production of new civilian product lines. Chapter 2 is devoted to an examination of the emerging economic theory of industrial organization and diversification. Readers more interested in policy may proceed directly to the country studies which begin in Chapter 3 without loss of continuity.

Notes

1. Bernard Udis, *From Guns to Butter: Technology Organizations and Reduced Military Spending in Western Europe* (Cambridge, MA: Ballinger Publishing Company, 1978).

2. This term is used here for convenience and should not be interpreted as either an endorsement or disparagement. "Industrial Policy" has been the subject of a long and continuing debate in the United States. Among the more prominent treatments are Barry Bluestone and Bennett Harrison, *The Deindustrialization of America* (New York, N.Y.: Basic Books, Inc. 1982), in favor; and Charles L. Schultze, "Industrial Policy: A Dissent," *The Brookings Review*, Fall 1983, pp. 3–12, opposed. Convenient summaries are found in Congressional Budget Office, *The Industrial Policy Debate* (Washington: Government Printing Office, December 1983); and "Industrial Policy: Is It The Answer?" *Business Week*, July 4, 1983, pp. 54–62. A deeper treatment which examines industrial maturity and market-generated renewal may be found in R.D. Norton, "Industrial Policy and American Renewal," *Journal of Economic Literature*, Vol. XXIV, No. 1, (March 1986), pp. 1–40.

3. The author was fortunate in having available three excellent studies which provide valuable details on such policies in Europe in supplementing his own field work. They are Lawrence Franko, *European Industrial Policy: Past, Present, and Future* (Brussels: Conference Board in Europe, 1980); Douglas Yuill and Kevin Allen (Eds.), *European Regional Incentives, 1984* (Glasgow: European Regional Policy Monitoring Unit, Centre For the Study of Public Policy, University of Strathclyde, 1984); and US International Trade Commission, *Foreign Industrial Targeting and Its Effect on US Industries, Phase II: The European Community and Member States*, Report to the Subcommittee on Trade, Committee on Ways and Means, US House of Representatives on Investigation No. 332–162 Under Section 332(b) of the Tariff Act of 1930 (Washington: US International Trade Commission Publication 1517, April 1984),

hereinafter referred to as Suomela, *et al.*, after Project Leader John W. Suomela and his research team.

4. In October 1985 Fairchild announced a plan to withdraw from its joint venture with Saab to produce the SF-340 commercial aircraft. Fairchild exchanged its prior role as equal partner with Saab for that of subcontractor as it moved to phase out of the venture completely by mid-1987. The decision was part of a plan by Fairchild to discontinue its aircraft operations in the hope of ending current losses by concentrating on its electronics and communications lines. See "Fairchild Will Take Pre-tax Charge of $100 Million, Leave Saab Venture," *Wall Street Journal*, October 18, 1985, p. 9.

5. There is some evidence that such policies may be interpreted in a more pliant way to aid some industries through difficult times. Thus, a West German executive noted, "Even our strict arms export regulations are handled by the government in a more flexible manner to allow, for instance, for export of submarines and frigates."

6. Kenneth E. Boulding, "The Impact of the Defense Industry on the Structure of the American Economy," in Bernard Udis (ed.), *The Economic Consequences of Reduced Military Spending* (Lexington, MA: Lexington Books, D.C. Heath and Company, 1973), pp. 225–252, especially p. 237.

7. A similar point is made by McGeorge Bundy, George F. Kennan, Robert McNamara and Gerard Smith, "Nuclear Weapons and the Atlantic Alliance," *Foreign Affairs*, Vol. 60, No. 4 (Spring, 1982), pp. 753–768, especially pp. 759–761. This point is emphasized even more strongly by a group of West German observers responding to the Bundy, *et al.* paper. See Karl Kaiser, Georg Leber, Alois Mertes, Franz-Josef Schulze, "Nuclear Weapons and the Preservation of Peace," *Foreign Affairs*, Vol. 60, No. 5 (Summer 1982), pp. 1157–1170, especially pp. 1164–1165.

TABLE 1.1 FRANCE: Major Elements of Industrial Policy, Pre-1974,
1974-1978, and Policymakers' Priorities in 1979-80

Pre-1974	1974-1978	1979-1980
Encourage concentration and mergers of national firms, often with the intention of blocking foreign takeovers.	Maintain employment by subsidies and low-interest loans to steel shipbuilding, auto, and machine tool companies.	Remove price controls to permit firms to have larger investable surpluses.
Promote high-technology industries by:	Push for EEC crisis cartels in steel, oil refining, and petrochemicals.	Allow bankruptcies (to eliminate inefficient management).
• Government investments in "national champions;" • Prestige Projects; • Gradually reversing the Gaullist policy of excluding foreign firms.	Partial nationalization of steel industry.	Legislate to control mergers and promote competition.
	Major export promotion effort, via:	Promote "Sectors of the Future," e.g., nuclear energy, aircraft, energy conservation electronic data processing, telecommunications by:
	• Loan guarantees; • Low interest credits for export sales and for capacity enlargement in export-oriented industries (10 billion FF in 1976, 3 billion in 1977); • Foreign policy support especially for aircraft and nuclear power sales.	• State investments; • Government purchasing; • Low interest loans; • Subsidies and tax incentives to user; • Soliciting and giving tax incentives to foreign (especially US) firms to form joint ventures; • Establishment of special funds for employment creation in troubled areas; • Employment creation by rebates of social charges to hiring firms.
	The oil price effect on the balance of payments is seen as a major constraint on French growth; energy policy is placed in the industry ministry headed by a former atomic energy chief. Establishment of CIASI to rescue ailing firms.	Reorient savings toward industry by tax deductions for share purchases. Increased consultation with labor. "Hard line" energy conservation. Emphasize public R&D support for industrial needs and small small business creation.

Source: Franko, 1980, p. 6.

TABLE 1.2 WEST GERMANY: Major Elements of Industrial Policy, Pre-1974,
1974-1978, and Policymakers' Priorities in 1979-80

Pre-1974	1974-1978	1979-1980
Increase federal R&D funding via new science and technology ministry.	Reduction in immigrant labor force.	Increase federal funding for R&D, especially in microelectronics and cooperative European aerospace ventures.
Some subsidization and protection for coal mines and shipbuilding, but also promotion of rationalization (capacity shrinkage and productivity improvements) through mergers.	Export promotion, trebling of government financing of capital goods exports, and doubling of amount of HERMES export insurance.	Funding of user firms to promote adoption of new technology (e.g., data processing).
Very large federal and Lander regional development aid, via grants, low cost loans, and tax concessions.	Introduction of "Innovation Premium" on labor costs of R&D (higher for smaller enterprises).	Creation of a special joint federal-Lander 5 billion DM fund (spread over 5 years) for the reconversion of the Ruhr region.
Involvement of labor unions in restructuring at company level through codetermination.	Reluctant participation in EEC crisis cartel in steel.	Major increase (20% over 1978-79 levels) in public support for R&D for coal liquefaction and gasification; 6 billion DM to be allocated annually.
Some public procurement preferences for high technology German industries.	Subsidies to shipbuilding sector (government pays 20% of cost of new ships), but companies basically forced to diversify, subcontracting out workers to survive.	Continuing subsidies to shipbuilding; loan guarantees for shipowners.
Participation in European-wide projects in aerospace and nuclear energy.		
Government credit guarantees for new small business of up to 80% of financing needs.	Special program of capital grants to encourage investment in regions affected by Volkswagen layoffs.	Support for foreign oil exploration by German companies in the DEMINEX consortium.
Favoring of mergers until 1973, (but Merger Control Law enacted that year required clearance of mergers resulting in firms with over 250 million DM in annual sales).	3 billion DM yearly fund to promote labor mobility (training, moving expenses, etc.).	

Source: Franko, 1980, p. 7.

TABLE 1.3 SWEDEN: Major Elements of Industrial Policy, Pre-1974,
1974-1978, and Policymakers' Priorities in 1979-80

Pre-1974	1974-1978	1979-1980
Ministry of Industry established in 1968, after commitment to "active industrial policy" announced by Social Democratic government in 1967 (state investment bank, Statsforetag state holding company, and board for technical development set up). Sectorial development program for industries in difficulty (e.g., textiles, shoes, furniture, and foundries).	Shift to major support of industries in trouble (subsidies to steel, shipbuilding, and shipowners). Large state loan guarantees to shipbuilding (85% of total support to industry in 1977). Nationalization of shipbuilding; participation in steel, (e.g., 1/3 ownership of a new group). More support and some subsidies for textiles, shoes and clothing (including 10% of wage cost for employees aged over 50); but these sectors already much reduced in size. Some success in cutting capacity (1/3 cut in shipbuilding 1973-76). Minor support to pulp, paper, and other wood products sectors. R&D support limited and declining (30% of total industry R&D including defense).	Ongoing debate between advocates of macroeconomic correctives (e.g., exchange rate devaluation) and those who favor industrial policy other than occasional rescue operations. Continued support to shipbuilding, steel, and textiles. Additional measures to promote labor mobility (moving expenses, job search grants, etc.). Modest increases in public R&D funding, small business loans, and promotion of large export consortia.

Source: Franko, 1980, p. 12.

TABLE 1.4 THE UNITED KINGDOM: Major Elements of Industrial Policy,
Pre-1974, 1974-1978, and Policymakers' Priorities in 1979-80

Pre-1974	1974-1978	1979-1980
Export promotion. Support for "national champion" companies against the "American challenge." Promote mergers and industrial concentration. Aids to less developed, less industrialized regions. Maintain employment in industries in difficulty by nationalization, current subsidies, and investment grants.	Maintain employment in industries in trouble via: • Current subsidies; • Regional aids to industrialized regions. Protection from import competition by national or EEC non-tariff barriers or cartel accords. Restructure industries in difficulty via: • Government investment grants; • Subsidies conditional on gradual reductions in capacity and labor force. Modest attempt to promote "industries of the future" by filling in equity/venture capital market for new ventures via the National Enterprise Board (but this never more than 10% of total NEB activity). Promote exports and stabilize import penetration (or reverse it) by developing a pro-productivity labor-management consensus in National Economic Development Council sector working parties.	New Conservative government emphasizing creation of a "favorable climate" (through anti-inflation monetary stringency, tax changes, elimination of price and exchange control) and officially de-emphasizing microeconomic interventions. Drive to cut public expenditure (hitting mainly sectorially non-selective regional grants—cut by 1/3). Subsidies to shipbuilding and steel being phased out, not eliminated. Sale of part of equity in profitable state enterprises to the private sector. Renewed commitment to state supported nuclear power development. National Enterprise Board venture capital entrepreneurial role downplayed, but a new £ 30 million NEB investment in titanium production for aircraft approved in absence of willingness to invest by private enterprise. Proposed competition bill attacks only anticompetitive abuses, not mergers. Continuation of (small) Labor government schemes to promote adaptation of microprocessor technology by British firms. Autonomous regional (e.g. Scottish) initiatives to promote inward investment by high technology foreign multinationals.

Source: Franko, 1980, p. 10.

TABLE 1.5 BELGIUM: Major Elements of Industrial Policy, Pre–1974,
1974–1978, and Policymakers' Priorities in 1979–80

Pre–1974	1974–1978	1979–1980
Attract foreign investment by capital grants and tax incentives.	Maintain employment at a reduced level by partial nationalization (steel) with provision of funds for rationalization and productivity improvements.	Maintain existing promotion instruments (industrial expansion laws).
Promote mergers and concentration of national firms.		To the extent permitted by regional, linguistic and political tensions, re-restructure the industrial sector along the lines of minister Claes' "New Industrial Policy" by providing administrative assistance in:
Promote general industrial expansion through low interest loans and investment premiums for increases in capacity and employment, but not restructuring (industrial expansion laws of 1959 and 1960).	Offer small interest free loans to firms preserving employment (Safeguard Plan of 1977). Promote the tightening of the Multifiber Agreement to protect the clothing and textile industries.	• Locating technology transfer opportunities; • Developing exports to non-traditional markets; • R&D coordination from concept to application; • Selective government purchasing; • Increasing the commercial scale of business; • Concentrating promotion efforts on selected projects.
		For the coordination and implementation of this policy, the creation of: • A fund for industrial renewal projects; • A state secretariat to concert sectorial policies, reinforcing traditional business-labor-government cooperation.

Source: Franko, 1980, p. 5.

TABLE 1.6 THE NETHERLANDS: Major Elements of Industrial Policy,
Pre-1974, 1974-1978, and Policymakers' Priorities in 1979-80

Pre-1974	1974-1978	1979-1980
Cash grants, large state loan guarantees, tax and other incentives to attract investment (often foreign) to less-developed regions.	Large sums spent on restructuring several sectors, including shipbuilding (e.g., current subsidies to cover current losses, and loan guarantees to promote mergers). 30% capacity reduction planned for shipbuilding.	Continued support of the measures provided for by the 1978 Investment Account Law.
	Extensive subsidies to promote employment of disadvantaged job seekers, and to save employment in individual companies, notably in textiles.	Modest increased government funding especially for development and use of energy saving and environmental protection technologies.
	Promote new industrial investment through general, regional, and small business investment premiums. Large income tax rebates and cash grants planned into the 1980's. (Investment Account Law of May 1978.)	Promote restructuring of, and moves away from, declining sectors by: • Increasing the transparency of subsidies; • Improving business-labor-government social consensus through the Restructuring Board.
	Export promotion measures, including some tying of previously untied aid to developing countries, low cost loans and guarantees (which doubled in volume between 1973 and 1977.)	Some export promotion, (e.g., subsidies and guarantees for preparation of bids on turnkey projects).
	Formation of joint business-labor-government Restructuring Board (NEHEM).	
	Continued aid to less developed regions (e.g., the North) through regional development companies.	

Source: Franko, p. 9.

TABLE 1.7   ITALY: Major Elements of Industrial Policy, Pre-1974,
1974-1978, and Policymakers' Priorities in 1979-80

Pre-1974	1974-1978	1979-1980
Promote private indus-trial development in the South via: • Capital grants; • Low-cost loans (state enterprises were obliged by statute to invest in the South); • Creation of GEPI, a a state holding company for rescue and salvage opera-tions; • Some minor promotion of mergers and con-solidations of Italy's very small scale enterprises via offers of low interest loans, etc.; • Some use of state enterprises to make counter-bids for local firms which were targets of foreign multinationals.	State takeovers (and in-creases in share parti-cipation) of failing companies plus subsidies and loans to maintain employment, especially in steel, clothing, ship-building, and chemicals. Capital grants and low cost loans for indus-trial development and employment in the South, and a slight shift from favoring capital-inten-sive industries. Move to restrict GEPI and other rescue opera-tions to the South (with indirect effect of forc-ing very rapid adjust-ment in the North).	Apply 3-year plan which has the first comprehensive framework for the state enterprise sector. With-drawal of support of govern-ment by the communists has however, delayed application and makes future measures unclear. Even greater emphasis on investment promotion in the South than in the past. Key elements of plan: • Replace short-term loans and current subsidies in state enterprises with large capital con-tributions (estimated at $3.6 billion in 1978-1981); • Limit further acquisitions by state enterprises to safeguard dynamism of private companies, es-pecially highly successful small- and medium-sized firms. Stated aim of GEPI rescue operations is to return firms to private sector; • Large state loans and grants (primarily to state companies) for electronics, telecommunications and data processing development; • Continued welcome of joint ventures by state firms with higher-technology multinationals.

Source: Franko, 1980, p. 8.

2

The Economics
of Diversification

For one who studies the process of resource transfer from military to civil uses ("economic conversion") a major source of frustration is the absence of a theoretical framework for analysis. While there has been much talk of "meeting unmet" societal needs with the impressive technology of the aerospace and electronics industries and a fair bit of questioning of just how serious military producers are about finding alternative products, there has been little systematic analysis of the conversion issue within the context of industrial diversification—which is, I believe, where it belongs.

Background

In a personal conversation with the author some years ago, an Italian industrialist observed that one of the most difficult decisions facing advanced technology firms operating in military markets is deciding how to commercialize promising new processes or products. Several routes are possible. The innovating firm may attempt to utilize the new innovation directly in its own operations. Alternatively, it may offer it to others via royalty or license arrangements. Here the familar "make or buy" decision facing all firms becomes more a question of "use or license."

In the intervening years since that conversation, two relevant parallel developments have been underway; one in the industrial world and the other in academic literature. The first of these has been the pervasive movement toward industrial diversification via internal growth and/or mergers of previously independent firms. In the early years of the movement in the 1960s, the diversifying firms appeared to be little constrained by considerations of unifying themes as the conglomerate merger movement seemed to sweep up firms producing in virtually all areas. One of the more unrestrained expressions of optimism in those years was the 1972 remark of G. William Miller, then president of Textron, Inc.: "I understand how to control manufacturing costs, but I'd be at a loss to control some of these service outfits that have 347 locations and no 'things'."[1] Presumably, Mr.

Miller had confidence in his firm's ability to manufacture almost any tangible product profitably.

While Textron may have been an extreme case, there is firm evidence that in the United States, at least, the entry of manufacturing firms into new fields by diversification has been substantial during the 1950–1975 period. Using Federal Trade Commission data sets (the "Corporate Patterns" survey for 1950 sales of the thousand largest manufacturing firms and the "Line of Business" survey for 1975 from 471 large corporations), Scherer and Ravenscraft studied data of a group of 200 US firms with the largest manufacturing product sales (value of shipments). Their figures disclose that in 1950, half of the top 200 firms indicated manufacturing activity in three or fewer lines of business but by 1975, only 10% were that restricted. The median number of reporting lines of business grew from 3.5 in 1950 to 9 in 1975, while mean values indicate a rough doubling in degree of diversification among the 200 largest manufacturers of 1950 when compared to the 200 largest in 1975.[2] Smaller companies demonstrated more pronounced increases in diversification than did the largest firms and consequently the clear difference in diversification by size of firm observed in 1950 had faded by 1975.[3] While no clear size-related pattern appeared among firms adding product lines through internal growth, diversification via acquisition was much more common among the smaller of the 200 largest companies of 1950. About half of their 1975 product lines were added by acquisition.[4]

While the "go-go" days of conglomerate mergers are behind us now, mergers and their undoings are still front page items in the financial press. Within one month in the summer of 1985, two cover stories in *Business Week* dealt with this subject[5] while *Fortune* was questioning whether General Motors could successfully handle its acquisitions of Electronic Data Systems (EDS) and Hughes Aircraft.[6] Two relatively recent articles in the US press also featured glowing acccounts of two important Swedish firms, Saab-Scania and Bofors, presumably because of their movement away from what might be viewed as "excessive" diversification and back toward concentration upon basics or what they know best.[7]

One searches in vain in such stories however, for clues as to the causes or determinants of successful diversification. *Business Week* cautions against the following "seven deadly sins" in mergers and acquisitions:

1. paying too much,
2. assuming a boom market won't crash,
3. leaping before looking,
4. straying too far afield,
5. swallowing something too big,
6. marrying disparate corporate cultures,
7. counting on key managers staying.[8]

However, what constitutes "too much, too far, too big, or disparate" can presumably only be determined ex-post.

The Economics of Organization:
An Academic Underworld

All this corporate scurrying to and fro has not elicited much interest within the ranks of academic economists with the possible exception of those concerned about the possible anti-trust implications. This may be attributed to the main line tradition of classical microeconomics of treating the firm as a "production function to which a profit-maximization objective has been assigned."[9] This view essentially ignores questions of internal organization. As Nelson puts it, traditional theory views the firm first, as a unit; second, as demonstrating behavior which is subjectively rational (in that the firm has some objectives and reasons for doing what it is doing); and third, as able to reliably and efficiently operate a variety of technologies available to most other firms. Thus, industry behavior can be modeled assuming the behavior of a typical firm. The theory therefore views the firm as essentially a "competent clerk" following predetermined, routinized behavior rules.[10] Further, since we take technologies, resources, and demands as given, the decision making clerks are essentially interchangeable.[11] Such a picture of firm behavior would appear inadequate to characterize the experimenting, error making, partial correcting, and insightful or blind behavior that marks major R&D activities when firms attempt things they have not done before.[12] If this kind of groping and stumbling is an apt description of the military producer attempting to enter new and unfamiliar markets, then the classical theory of the firm would appear to offer little guidance or understanding of the process.

The fundamental questions asked by Coase, "What determines what a firm does? Why isn't General Motors a dominant factor in the coal industry, or why doesn't A & P manufacture airplanes?"[13] are most relevant to the economic conversion question. Coase moved away from traditional theory by rejecting the view that the limits of the firm were a parameter and by arguing that the firm's limits were themselves a decision variable requiring economic evaluation. The issue requiring attention is the identification of "efficient boundaries" for the firm so that questions of what activities should be performed within the firm, which outside it, and why, can be answered.[14]

Recent developments in the theory of transaction costs and economies of scope have substantially advanced our ability to define efficient boundaries. The most fundamental work is that of Williamson,[15] and Baumol, Panzar, and Willig.[16] An important extension is provided by Teece.[17]

Transaction Costs

The transaction cost approach to the study of economic organization focuses on the transaction as the basic unit of interest, in contrast with commodities. It further recognizes that alternative governance structures exist for the organization of economic activity with the two principal types being the firm and the market. The choice is assumed to be influenced primarily by the goal of economizing on transaction costs. Williamson describes transaction costs as the economic equivalent to friction on mechanical systems and suggests the necessity for a comparative analysis of the costs of "planning, adapting, and monitoring task completion under alternative governance structures."[18]

In a recent paper, Gordon criticized the new classical models of price adjustment and macroeconomic disturbances for their failure to recognize the *"pervasive heterogeneity* in types and quality of products, and in the location and timing of transations."[19] (Emphasis in the original.) He goes on to stress the role of transaction costs in explaining market structure.[20] While we might cite other converts to the transaction cost approach to contracting, Riordan and Williamson caution that it "does not threaten to become the new orthodoxy."[21] However, once the traditional focus on steady-state production costs is expanded to include transaction costs, a valuable tool becomes available to help understand the choice of organizational or administrative structure.[22]

Williamson has noted that transaction cost economizing by itself is incomplete and needs to be placed within a larger economizing framework which would recognize the production cost consequences.[23] I believe the development of the concept of economies of scope or "trans-ray convexity" is a clear move in that direction.

Economies of Scope

The term, "economies of scope," was coined by Panzar and Willig to describe cost savings which derive from the scope of operations of the firm in contrast to their scale.[24] When present, such economies suggest that two or more product lines can be produced more cheaply within a firm than separately. Multiproduct firms are a likely consequence of scope economies. While the term is new, its minters concede their debt to economists of an earlier era (Clark and Clemens) who suggested that the multiproduct firm was a likely outgrowth of some form of excess capacity. More recently, Casson has focused on under-utilized managerial capacity as a source of diversification.[25] Panzar and Willig speak of a sharable, "quasi public input whose services can be shared by two or more product lines without complete congestion."[26] An input is defined "as sharable between the productions of product sets S and T if the joint production of these outputs enables some of the input to be conserved, vis-a-vis separate production, while the utilizations of all other inputs were not expanded."[27] The concept of "subadditivity" is also introduced; a condition where the costs of providing the services of the sharable input to two or more product lines are less than the total costs of providing these services separately to each product line.[28]

Trans-ray Convexity

Baumol, Panzar, and Willig (BPW) introduce a similar indicator of complementarity in production called, "trans-ray convexity" which can be shown as a cross section of a cost hypersurface that connects points on the output axes.[29] Figures 2.1 and 2.2 illustrate two shapes which such a cross section might take above line segment RT. Points R and T are on the y1 and y2 axes, respectively. Following from the fact that a line segment such as RT must be perpendicular to some ray in the y1 y2 plane, BPW refer to the segment of the cost surface above RT as a trans-ray cross section.

This cross section may be used to compare the costs of specialized firms at such points as R and T on the axes with those of firms producing a weighted average of the two outputs. A move toward the center of RT represents a reduction in the level of specialization in the activities of the firm, and in the circumstances shown in Figure 2.1 (trans-ray convexity), a reduction in its costs as well. Thus, in Figure 2.1, since the cross section curves downward toward the center, multiproduct production is relatively cheaper than specialized production. Using the numbers shown in Figure 2.1, specialized production of R costs 2000 and of point T, 6000. For the midpoint however, $C(S)=2500<1/2\ C(R)+1/2\ C(T)=4000$.

Figure 2.2 illustrates the opposite circumstances. Here, multiproduct production is associated with relative cost disadvantage. Graphically this is shown by the upward curvature of the cross section toward the center of the diagram. Arithmetically, $C(S)=4500$ is larger than a weighted average of the costs resulting from specialized production at points R and T.

BPW note that their formal definition of trans-ray convexity refers to a particular output vector; y. Thus, the cost surface may be trans-ray convex at one point but not satisfy the condition at another point. Of particular interest is their suggestion that near the origin of the diagram there may be cross sections like that in Figure 2.1 (trans-ray convex), but further out its trans-ray cross sections may be concave like that in Figure 2.2.[30] If such a condition existed in reality, it would suggest the economic limits of diversification.

Interaction of Transaction Costs and Scope Economies

In an interesting paper, Teece cautions that scope economies do not provide either a necessary or sufficient condition for cost savings to be attained through the merger of specialized firms.[31] He provides the interesting example of mixed farming where an orchardist utilizes the necessary space between fruit trees by planting grass and grazing sheep in the intervening pasture. He insists that while scope economies are present in the form of the common input, the resulting organizational implications are not equally clear since rather than undertaking jointly the production of fruit and sheep, the orchardist may lease the pasture to a sheep farmer. Here, a market contract is an alternative to the single diversified enterprise.[32]

Teece argues that to predict the organizational structure likely to result when economies of scope characterize the cost function, the origin of such scope economies must be known. His focus is placed upon the ease with which the common input or its services can be traded across markets. When such trading is difficult and intrafirm governance is superior, the multiproduct firm is likely to evolve. Teece sees only two types of common input where these conditions hold: know-how and specialized, indivisible physical assets. Even here, presence of such common inputs is not a sufficient condition for the evolution of the multiproduct enterprise.[33] Whether internal organization within the firm or market processes are utilized depends upon what Williamson has called the "three initial dimensions for characterizing transactions . . . 1) uncertainty, 2) the frequency with which transactions recur, and 3) the degree to which durable transaction-specific investments are incurred (investment idiosyncrasy)."[34]

With respect to uncertainty, Williamson has suggested that as the conduct of transactions approaches the more certain end of the continuum, the form of the government structure becomes less significant.[35] On the other hand, as the degree of uncertainty grows, a unified (internal) governance structure is likely to evolve to reduce the costs of resolving the increasing number of differences among the parties likely to accompany frequent change in an uncertain situation.

As regards the frequency of transactions, one might establish three classes: the discreet one-time transaction; an intermediate degree of frequency (occasional); and recurrent transactions. Since few transactions in the context of our interests are of the one-time variety, further attention will be limited to the occasional and recurrent.

These two characteristics of transactions—uncertainty and frequency— are of limited value in explaining governance form until they are linked to the third crucial characteristic; transaction-specific investments. In tracing out this model, Williamson notes that asset specificity can take three forms: 1) site specificity to economize on inventory and transport expenditures, 2) physical asset specificity as, for example, reliance on specialized dies, and 3) human asset specificity that develops in a learning-by-doing situation.[36]

The effect of the investment is to lock the buyer and seller into what is essentially a bilateral exchange condition for an extended period of time since the value of highly specific capital is greater in the use for which it was originally designed than in other applications. Thus, in the presence of substantial asset-specificity, both buyer and seller are motivated to develop an exchange relation with high probability of continuity and with firm contractual safeguards. Writing and implementing such contracts is expensive.

Williamson notes that internal direction within the firm yields three principal advantages over bilateral trade in the market. Thus, common ownership:

- offsets the incentive to suboptimize and pursue local goals
- provides fiat as a means to resolve disputes which would require expensive
- legal proceedings to settle similar disputes between independent traders
- provides easier and more complete access to necessary information when disputes require settlement[37]

Figure 2.3 represents Williamson's effort graphically to illustrate the heart of the above argument by representing both production cost differences and governance cost differences as functions of asset specificity (A). The figure is interpreted by having $\Delta C = f(a)$ represent production cost differences between internal organization and the market while $\Delta G = g(A)$ represents the corresponding governance cost difference. If the vertical sum of $\Delta C + \Delta G$ is positive, market procurement retains the advantage. When $\Delta C + \Delta G = 0$ (at $\hat{A}$), indifference prevails between governance structures. When values of A exceed $\hat{A}$, internal procurement is advantageous since $\Delta C + \Delta G < 0$ in this range.[38] In an interesting application to the real world, Williamson explains the acquisition of Fisher Body by General Motors in 1926 using these concepts.[39]

The Model Applied

Assuming an intermediate level of uncertainty, Williamson has suggested a matrix for the matching of governance structure with the form of transaction based upon the interaction of frequency of transaction and degree of specificity of investment.[40] It is reproduced as Figure 2.4. One immediately observes that unified, internal governance is most likely to evolve in recurrent transactions with idiosyncratic investment. For the purposes of this paper it is perhaps more useful to consider a modification of Williamson's matrix by Teece.[41] Figure 2.5 subjects the transfer of know-how to a similar analysis while Figure 2.6 indicates the likely resulting organizational forms.

This device could be highly useful in attempting to predict what types of diversification are most likely to lend themselves to a successful implementation by the developing firm and which probably would do better in an arm's length relationship between developer and user via royalty licensing.

Another area for the application of the framework is in the analysis of "offsets" or compensation in international trade. Under direct offset agreements as a condition of sale the buyer requires permission to produce a portion of the product domestically. One of the more well-publicized offset arrangements provided that industry in Belgium, The Netherlands, Denmark, and Norway would manufacture parts for the aggregate initial purchase of 998 F-16 aircraft (348 European and 650 US Air Force) which would approximate 58% of the value of the European order. Such offset demands have become quite important as a negotiating point in such international transactions. The analysis presented above provides a useful approach to understanding the willingness of firms to agree to such offsets. Where the principal contractor fulfills the role of designer or architect and assembler of the final product and standardized parts and sub-assemblies are routinely provided by other firms, offsets as a condition of sale are less likely to be resisted. This is because the participation of the foreign firm is most likely to come at the expense of domestic subcontractors rather than the prime contractor. This, in fact, seems to be the case in the aerospace and electronics industries where offsets are most frequently encountered.

Limits to Diversification

As noted above, even in theory, economies of scope do not necessarily operate without limit. Teece has also noted the likely presence of a congestion factor when simultaneous transfer of know-how to a variety of different applications is undertaken.[42] This results from the fact that knowledge frequently is not embodied completely in blueprints and documents but involves a human element as well. If the transfer involves a learning-by-doing component, human capital in the form of an effective team may be necessary with associated bottlenecks. Similarly, in the case of an indivisible specialized asset, scope economies which result from sharing that asset will be exhausted when the asset is fully utilized.

Summary

The challenge facing the management of militarily-dependent firms in their efforts to diversify may be described as that of defining efficient borders or limits to their activities. The concepts of transaction cost economizing and economies of scope provide useful guidance in meeting that challenge. As Teece argues, "diversification based on scope economies does not represent abandonment of specialization economies in favor of amorphous growth."[43] It reflects, rather, a redefinition of the firm's comparative advantage, shifting away from a focus on products to one based on capabilities. In his words, "The firm [establishes] a specialized know-how or asset base from which it extends its operations in response to competitive conditions."[44] This would appear to be a fair description of what Saab-Scania attempted when it established the new Combitech division to undertake the commercialization of innovations developed in its aircraft division. Here, certain familiar characteristics of the aerospace industry may be seen as encouraging scope economies. Such phenomena as a well-developed ability to deal with the contracting authorities of the government; a sizeable stock of scientists and engineers engaged in current production and maintained in anticipation of future contracts; and the high variability of production in the industry all argue for diversification and scope economies.[45]

It is traditional to close a survey effort of this sort by suggesting further avenues of research. I shall follow that tradition by advocating the testing of the hypotheses put forth here. This could be accomplished by classifying diversification efforts according to the schema provided in Figures 2.4 and 2.6 and by predicting the likely success of such efforts. Hopefully, this will take us further toward understanding the determinants of successful diversification than *Business Week's* seven deadly sins.

Notes

1. "Is Textron Ready for a Take Off?," *Business Week*, October 7, 1972, pp. 66–71, especially p. 68.

2. Frederic M. Scherer and David Ravenscraft, "Growth By Diversification: Entrepreneurial Behavior in Large-Scale United States Enterprises," *Zeitschrift fur Nationalokonomie,* Supplement 4, 1984, pp. 199–218, especially pp. 203–204.

3. Scherer and Ravenscraft, "Growth By Diversification: Entrepreneurial Behavior in Large-Scale United States Enterprises," pp. 204–205.

4. Scherer and Ravenscraft, "Growth By Diversification: Entrepreneurial Behavior in Large-Scale United States Enterprises," pp. 210–211.

5. "Do Mergers Really Work?," *Business Week,* June 3, 1985, pp. 88–100; and "Splitting Up," *Business Week,* July 1, 1985, pp. 50–55.

6. Michael Brody, "Can GM Manage It All?," *Fortune,* July 8, 1985, pp. 22–28.

7. Louis Richman, "Saab-Scania Kicks Into High Gear," *Fortune,* November 26, 1984, pp. 105–112; and Alan L. Otten, "Bofors of Sweden Shoots Back to Basics, Scores Bulls-Eye in Operating Earnings," *Wall Street Journal,* June 17, 1980, p. 19.

8. "Do Mergers Really Work?," *Business Week,* June 3, 1985, p. 90.

9. Oliver E. Williamson, "The Economics of Organization: The Transaction Cost Approach," *American Journal of Sociology,* Volume 87, Number 3 (November 1981), pp. 548–577, especially p. 548.

10. Richard R. Nelson, "Issues and Suggestions for the Study of Industrial Organization in a Regime of Rapid Technological Change," in Victor R. Fuchs (ed.), *Policy Issues and Research Opportunities in Industrial Organization* (New York: Columbia University Press, 1972), pp. 34–58, especially, pp. 35–37.

11. Nelson, "Issues and Suggestions for the Study of Industrial Organization in a Regime of Rapid Technological Change," p. 37.

12. Nelson, "Issues and Suggestions for the Study of Industrial Organization in a Regime of Rapid Technological Change," p. 38. Other distinguished economists have challenged the traditional static micro model of the firm during the past 25 years although there is little recognition of it in the standard textbooks. Such challenges include managerial discretion theory [William J. Baumol, *Business Behavior, Value, and Growth* (New York: Macmillian, 1959) and Robin Marris, *The Economic Theory of "Managerial" Capitalism* (New York: Free Press, 1964)]; team theory [Jacob Marschak and Roy A. Radner, *The Theory of Teams* (New Haven: Yale University Press, 1972)]; agency theory [Armen A. Alchian and Harold Demsetz, "Production, Information Costs, and Economic Organization," *American Economic Review,* Volume 62, Number 5 (December 1972), pp. 777–795; Michael C. Jensen and William H. Meckling, "Theory of the Firm: Managerial Behavior, Agency Costs and Ownership Structure," *Journal of Financial Economics,* Volume 3, Number 4 (October 1976), pp. 305–360]; and transaction cost theory [Ronald H. Coase, "The Nature of the Firm" in George J. Stigler and Kenneth E. Boulding (Eds.), *Readings in Price Theory* (Homewood, Illinois: Irwin, 1952), pp. 386–405; and Oliver E. Williamson, *Markets and Hierarchies* (New York: Free Press, 1975)].

13. Ronald H. Coase, "Industrial Organization: A Proposal for Research," in Victor H. Fuchs (ed.), *Policy Issues and Research Opportunities in Industrial Organization,* pp. 59–73, especially pp. 63 and 67.

14. Williamson, "The Economics of Organization," p. 549.

15. Williamson, Markets and Hierarchies; "Transaction-Cost Economics: The Governance of Contractual Relations," *The Journal of Law and Economics,* Volume 22, Number 2 (October 1979), pp. 233–261; "The Economics of Organization;" "The Modern Corporation: Origins, Evolution, Attributes," *Journal of Economic Literature,* Volume 19, Number 4 (December 1981), pp. 1537–1568; "The Incentive Limits of Firms: A Comparative Institutional Assessment of Bureaucracy," *Weltwirtschaftliches Archiv,* Band 120, Heft 4, 1984, pp. 736–763; and "Asset Specificity and Economic

Organization," with Michael H. Riordan, Working Paper Series D, #6 (New Haven: Yale University School of Organization and Management, May 1985).

16. William J. Baumol, John C. Panzar, and Robert D. Willig, *Contestable Markets and The Theory of Industry Structure* (New York: Harcourt Brace Jovanovich, Inc., 1982); also John C. Panzar and Robert D. Willig, "Economies of Scope," *American Economic Review*, Volume 71, Number 2 (May 1981), pp. 268–272.

17. David J. Teece, "Economies of Scope and the Scope of the Enterprise," *Journal of Economic Behavior and Organization*, Volume 1, Number 3 (September 1980), pp. 223–247.

18. Williamson, "The Economics of Organization," p. 553.

19. Robert J. Gordon, "Output Fluctuations and Gradual Price Adjustment," *Journal of Economic Literature*, Volume 19, Number 2 (June 1981), pp. 493–530, especially p. 517.

20. Gordon, "Output Fluctuations and Gradual Price Adjustment," pp. 517–519.

21. Riordan and Williamson, "Asset Specificity and Economic Organization," p. 3.

22. For example, I have used the transaction cost concept in a comparative analysis of the different approaches utilized to manage the production of two military aircraft produced on a collaborative basis: the MRCA-Tornado by the United Kingdom, Federal Republic of Germany, and Italy; and the F-16 by the United States, Belgium, the Netherlands, Norway, and Denmark. See Bernard Udis, "Lessons From Aerospace: The Prospects for Rationalization in NATO," *Orbis*, Volume 25, Number 1 (Spring 1981), pp. 165–196, especially pp. 180–182.

23. Williamson, "The Economics of Organization," p. 552.

24. Panzar and Willig, "Economies of Scope," p. 268.

25. Mark Casson, *The Entrepreneur: An Economic Theory* (Totowa, N.J.: Barnes and Noble Books, 1982), pp. 315–318. The role of fixed costs in explaining scope economies is emphasized in Ian E. Gorman, "Conditions for Economies of Scope in the Presence of Fixed Costs," *Rand Journal of Economics*, Vol. 16, No. 3 (Autumn 1985), pp. 431–436.

26. Panzar and Willig, "Economies of Scope," p. 270.

27. Panzar and Willig, "Economies of Scope," p. 269.

28. Panzar and Willig, "Economies of Scope," p. 268.

29. Baumol, Panzar, Willig, *Contestable Markets and The Theory of Industry Structure*, pp. 79–83.

30. Baumol, Panzar, Willig, *Contestable Markets and The Theory of Industry Structure*, p. 81.

31. Teece, "Economies of Scope and the Scope of the Enterprise," p. 225.

32. Teece, "Economies of Scope and the Scope of the Enterprise," p. 225.

33. Teece, "Economies of Scope and the Scope of the Enterprise," p. 226.

34. Williamson, "Transaction-Cost Economics," pp. 239–240.

35. Williamson, "Transaction-Cost Economics," pp. 253–254.

36. Williamson, "The Modern Corporation," p. 1546.

37. Williamson, "The Modern Corporation," p. 1549.

38. Williamson, "The Economics of Organization," p. 559.

39. Williamson, "The Economics of Organization," p. 561.

40. Williamson, "Transaction-Cost Economics," p. 253.

41. Teece, "Economies of Scope and the Scope of the Enterprise," pp. 230–231.

42. Teece, "Economies of Scope and the Scope of the Enterprise," pp. 232–233.

43. Teece, "Economies of Scope and the Scope of the Enterprise," p. 233.

44. Teece, "Economies of Scope and the Scope of the Enterprise," p. 233.

45. These final points were suggested by Loren Yager of the Aerospace Research Center of the Aerospace Industries Association of America, Inc.

Figure 2.1: Trans-Ray Convexity

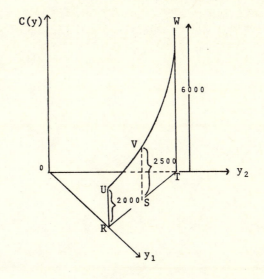

Source: Baumol, Panzar and Willig, pp. 79-80.

Figure 2.2: Trans-Ray Concavity

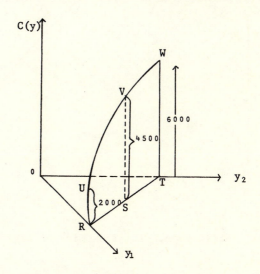

Source: Baumol, Panzar and Willig, pp. 79-80.

Figure 2.3: Net Production and Governance Cost Differences

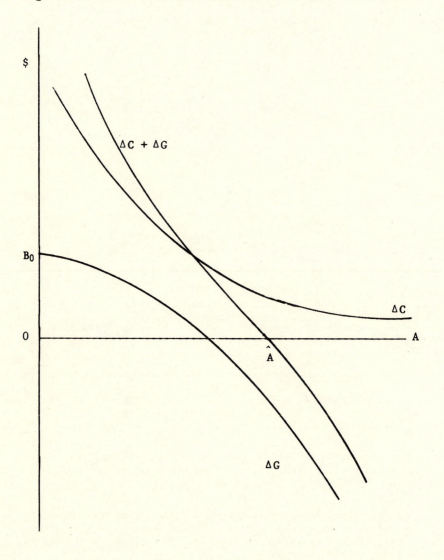

Source: Williamson, "The Economics of Organization," p. 560.

Figure 2.4:   Matching Governance Structures with Commercial
              Transactions

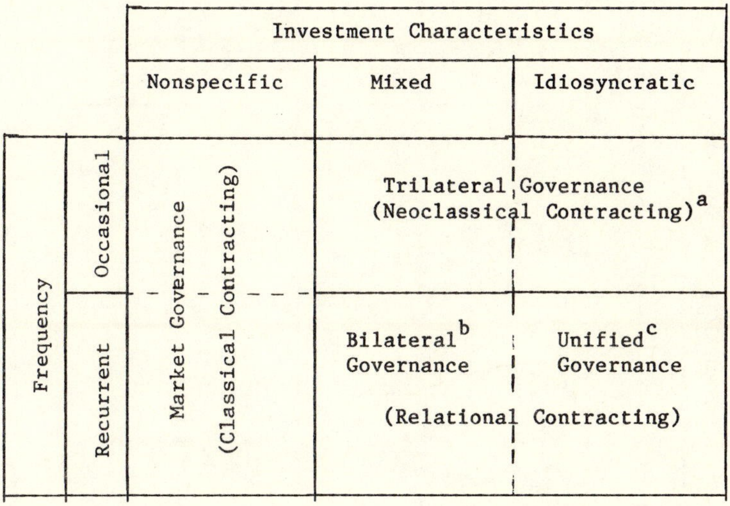

	Investment Characteristics		
	Nonspecific	Mixed	Idiosyncratic
Frequency — Occasional	Market Governance (Classical Contracting)	Trilateral Governance (Neoclassical Contracting)[a]	
Frequency — Recurrent	Market Governance (Classical Contracting)	Bilateral[b] Governance (Relational Contracting)	Unified[c] Governance (Relational Contracting)

Source: Williamson, "Transaction – Cost Economics," p. 253.

[a] Here strong incentives exist to having the contract run to
completion with market relief for failure to deliver both
expensive and generally unsatisfactory. Some form of third party
intervention or arbitration is preferred to the disrupting
consequences of litigation.

[b] An intermediate level of asset specialization may encourage
outside procurement to attain scale economy advantages. Hence
the autonomy of the parties is maintained.

[c] Increasingly idiosyncratic transactions weaken incentives for
trading in the market since as assets become more specialized,
economies of scale are as likely to be realized by the buyers as
by an outside supplier.

Figure 2.5: Know-How Transactions Characterized by Transaction Frequency and Proprietary Status

FREQUENCY OF TRANSFER	CHARACTERISTICS OF KNOW-HOW			
	NON PROPRIETARY		PROPRIETARY →	
	nonspecialized application	specialized application	nonspecialized application	specialized application
occasional →	transfer of standard engineering service for particular product or process	transfer of custom engineering service for particular product or process	transfer of "spin-off" technology with nonspecialized application	transfer of "spin-off" technology with specialized application
recurrent →	transfer of know-how for well known process (e.g., thermal cracking of petroleum)	application of well known process to new use (e.g., packaging technology modified for new product)	transfer of process know-how in standard formulation to firms in other markets (e.g., petroleum platforming technology)	transfer of know-how for specialized application in another industry (e.g., aircraft technology applied to aerospace development)

Source: Teece, p. 230.

Figure 2.6: Matching Governance Structures with Type of Know-How Transferred and Transaction Frequency

FREQUENCY OF CONTEMPLATED TRANSACTIONS	CHARACTERISTICS OF KNOW-HOW			
	NON PROPRIETARY		PROPRIETARY →	
	nonspecialized application	specialized application	nonspecialized application	specialized application
occasional	markets	markets	markets	markets
recurrent	markets	markets	obligational contracting / obligational contracting/intrafirm organization	obligational contracting/intrafirm organization / intrafirm organization

Source: Teece, p. 231.

3

France

In industrial policy, as in so many other areas, France is a case unto itself. It has pursued an active industrial policy longer than almost any other state and that policy is an outgrowth of its unique history and institutions. French government intervention to encourage the growth of new industries and technologies has a long tradition which in the view of a French economist is explained by two principal conditions:

1. France has been unified and centralized longer than most other European states and an uninterrupted powerful centralized administration can be traced back to the 18th century. As a text-book example of mercantilism, intervention in the economy and industrial policy have long been traditional means to secure such national goals as security, independence, wealth, and prestige.

2. France, as a Latin and Catholic country, lacked capitalist trading traditions found among its Protestant neighbors and was dominated by a propertied aristocratic class. After the expulsion of its Protestant merchant class in the 18th century the wealthy preferred to invest in land or government bonds rather than in trade and industry, and generally demonstrated risk-averse behavior. Therefore, government initiatives, presumably, were necessary to take the place of the missing private ventures, particularly in sectors characterized by advanced technology and large capital requirements.[1]

Jean Baptiste Colbert, minister to Louis XIV of France, has been identified as the first global and consistent industrial strategist, and his name has become symbolic of such a strategy—*Colbertism*. In any event, his policies combined protection from foreign competition with incentives (grants of monopoly and patents, subsidies, and training programs) to develop advanced technology and modern industry in France.[2]

It is of interest to note that the favored industries were those closely related to military production—gun foundries and battleship yards.

Some important institutions formed to administer such policies continue to play important roles today. These include the government technical schools which still provide the several corps of state engineers with their well-trained personnel. The Saint-Simonian movement of the nineteenth century also stressed close links between dynamic entrepreneurs and bankers and the government to aid the development of that period's promising new industries: coal mining, pig-iron and steel production, steamships, waterways, and railroads. From 1850 to 1870 France experienced a high-growth rate of output and of investment. From the end of that period to World War II France reverted to economic protectionism and by 1940 more than a third of the French working population was located in agriculture. Despite some technological gains, conservative small and undersized-firms dominated French industry.

Post–World War II Planning[3]

By War's end, French industry was largely destroyed and the output level at less than half the 1913 level. However, the economic recovery was truly remarkable and in the 1946–1973 period the French growth rate became the most rapid in the European Economic Community (EEC). In the early postwar years, indicative planning and nationalization of key organizations were utilized to direct funds for investment into strategic sectors (coal, hydroelectricity, steel, cement, chemicals, etc.). During the Gaullist regime in the 1960s new government ventures were begun to provide France with independence in the technologies underlying aircraft, space, nuclear weapons and energy, oil drilling and refining, computers, and electronics. The following decade saw their development and success in export markets, and additional government-supported projects in nuclear electricity, telecommunications, and electronics.

French indicative planning involves the use of a loose system of government initiatives, and is based on consultation among representatives of industry, unions, government agencies, and the Planning Commission. Although the plans are not binding, their objectives are pursued by the government's use of administrative guidance, credit, subsidies, and taxation. The first three plans covering the period 1946–1961 dealt principally with restoring the war-damaged economy and removing supply bottlenecks. The fourth plan (1959–1965) established economy-wide investment goals and a strategy for growth. Its degree of detail was substantially increased, which has been attributed to the growing importance of foreign trade since the economy had previously been rather protected from foreign competition. The tariff reductions expected to flow from the Kennedy round of trade negotiations and the trade liberalization of the European Community may have been taken as signs of an enhanced need for government intervention.[4]

The fifth plan (1966–1970) focused on correcting perceived weaknesses in the French economy which were seen as retarding its ability to compete with US-based multinational firms. Its authors attributed French industrial weakness to lower growth rates of investment and the smaller size of French firms relative to foreign competitors. To correct these problems, the plan encouraged mergers and cartels, exempted particular firms from regulations viewed as discouraging investment and outlays on research and development, and focused investment in certain advanced-technology areas. The last policy resulted in the promotion of one or two firms of substantial size in each industry. These "national champions" which could be public or private, depending on the industry, would receive R&D grants, public orders, etc., to encourage scale economies in their operations.

The sixth and seventh plans, which spanned the 1971–1980 period, were somewhat less sweeping and provided for state intervention in such high-technology areas as computers, electronics, telecommunications machinery, and chemicals.

The Concorde SST, Airbus, and high-speed trains were included in their results, technologically impressive if not profitable. Less successful at either level were the Plans Calcul and Siderurge—the first to develop a leading world computer industry and the second to nationalize and update the steel industry.

The eighth and current plan (1981–1985) was somewhat delayed by the change in administrations following the Socialist electoral victory in 1981. Interim plans released in 1982 and 1983 reaffirm the goals of modernizing basic industry, improving competitiveness in process industries and advancing new technologies.

Nationalization of Enterprises

While direct government ownership of industry and banking companies predates World War II, it accelerated in the immediate post-war period, initially as punishment for those who collaborated with the Vichy regime and the Germans during the war. The 1944–1947 nationalization wave saw the electricity, gas and coal industries, the Bank of France, the main commercial banks and insurance companies, and the Renault automobile company join the ranks of the nationalized. However, government intervention in France has progressed well beyond the nationalized sector via its trade, tax, finance, and competitive policies.

During the Gaullist period in the 1960s, new public enterprises were developed to serve as the instruments of an industrial policy identified as the "grandes projects." These included Elf-Aquitaine in oil, Societe Nationale Industrielle Aerospatiale in aerospace, Compagnie Internationale pour l'Informatique in information technology, and Comega in nuclear materials.

The third major wave of nationalization in this century occurred in 1981 following the political victory of the Socialist Party under Francois Mitterand. Twelve major companies and the remaining private banks were added to the nationalized sector which now controls about 25% of manufacturing and about half of the highly-concentrated oligopoly sector. Thus, nationalized enterprises now run the major part of basic industry (steel, metals, chemicals, materials, etc.), and most of the advanced-technology equipment sector (aerospace, electronics, telecommunications, heavy engineering, etc.).[5]

While largely autonomous in routine management decisions, the nationalized firms operate under the guidance of the government ministries. Long-term strategy is negotiated with the state within the framework of what are called "planning contracts." The companies receive public loans and capital from the Budget Ministry and banking sector to finance their investment and research strategies. Government-supplied capital is provided to encourage the nationalized firms to assume long-term risks and to invest countercyclically. The process has been costly. In 1982 only one of the companies (Compagnie Generale d'Electricite) earned a profit. In 1982 and 1983 government contributions to the twelve nationalized groups were the equivalent of $1.3 and $2.3 billion, respectively, with the largest amounts going to enterprises in steel, chemicals, and autos. Since the 1981 nationalizations, government industrial policy has become more direct, and the pre-existing encouragement of high technology industry has been broadened to include modernization of older basic industries. The French government has demonstrated substantial political courage in pursuing modernization plans, such as that for the steel industry, which will result in the loss of thousands of jobs. The political acceptability of such a program will depend in no small way on the operations of the unemployment compensation system, retraining arrangements, and plans to increase the mobility of capital and labor (topics to be discussed below).

Instruments of Industrial Policy[6]

If the goals of current French policy described above are to be attained, it will require large increases in government outlays for research and development and the provision of financial resources by the newly-nationalized banking sector to the industries targeted for modernization and development. The government may have to be the customer of last resort through public procurement in some cases and to actively encourage exports in others. This suggests a continuation of the government's delicately-balanced effort to discourage certain imports, and to encourage foreign investment where it brings France access to important foreign technologies.

Government laboratories and research centers in the applied sciences also constitute tools of industrial policy. Most of these were created or significantly expanded under the policy of Charles de Gaulle to expand national independence. Among the more important are the CEA (Commissariat a l'Energie Atomique) which develops materials and engineering; the CNES (Centre National de'Etudes Spatiales) which develops space launchers and satellites; the CNET (Centre National d'Etudes des Telecommunications) which works on advanced telecommunications; and others which operate in such fields as oceanography, biology, information technology, etc.

The Ministry of Research and Technology had been responsible until recently for the development of the budgets of the government laboratories and research centers and an important goal had been to ensure that long-term program continuity was not sacrificed to short-term fiscal pressures.[7] Other government ministries also play important roles in support of industrial policy. Thus, the Treasury regulates financial markets aided by the nationalized banks. It also controls the debt strategy of the principal public enterprises, and provides public loans or capital endowments to industry—both public and private. The Budget and Foreign Trade Departments monitor industrial subsidies and export promotion loans.

The technical ministries and their staffs significantly influence industrial strategy. The degree of such influence is a function of its links with those industries with which it interacts. Thus, close relations exist between the Ministry of Defense (MOD) and the armaments firms, or between the Ministry of Post and Telecommunications and the telecommunications and electronics industries. Public procurement also provides ministries with the ability to influence such crucial industrial decisions as technical standards for equipment, price levels, export strategy, etc. Nationalized firms in manufacturing, energy, and transport are obviously influenced by the Ministries of Industry and Transportation.

The ministries are staffed by a crack professional group of civil servants whose careers are highly stable and who operate in a corps attached to a ministry. This limits the number and influence of political appointees, especially in the technical ministries. The "Grandes Ecoles," specialized establishments of higher education, provide the professional staff of the several corps. It is interesting to note that these schools are operated by the ministries and not by the University system. Recruitment to the schools is via a system of tough competitive examinations, which attract the best students since the graduates of the Grandes Ecoles are viewed as the class which runs France.

Graduates of the Ecole Nationale d'Administration staff the administrative and diplomatic corps. The scientific and engineering schools probably play a larger role in industrial policy. Among these are the Ecole Polytechnique, founded in 1794 and its ecoles d'application which provide high-level technical training for the several corps of state engineers. The Ecole de Mines and the Corps des Mines supply staff for the ministries of industry and of the energy and basic industry sectors. The Ecole and Corps des Ponts et Chaussees play a similar role for the ministries of Public Works, Urban Development and Transportation; the Ecole and Corps de l'Armament for Defense, the Ecole and Corps des Telecommunications for PTT (Post, Telephone, Telegraph), etc.

Typically, public enterprises and government research centers are managed by former technical civil servants and graduates of the Grandes Ecoles. The same background is often encountered among those holding the top positions of private firms. This results in a ". . . close interpenetration of administrative and industrial technocracies [which] has no equivalent in the Western World, not even in Japan. More than any other factor, that interconnection helps to explain the close coordination and mutual trust which exists between administrative and industrial strategies in key sectors."[8]

Regional Policy[9]

The French regional incentive system was thoroughly revised in May 1982. Two new financial incentives—a regional policy grant and a regional employment grant—were introducted to replace the earlier set of six programs. The programs withdrawn were a regional development grant, PDR; a special fund for industrial adaptation, FSAI; a service location grant, PLAT; a research location grant, PLAR; a special rural aid, ASR; and a decentralization subsidy. The financial components of the aid package remain a local business tax concession, a special depreciation allowance, and a reduction in property transfer tax.

The principal regional aid in France is the regional policy grant (prime d'amenagement du territoire, PAT), a project-related grant to manufacturing firms and to research and service sector activities. It integrates into one program what previously existed in three: the PDR (which covered manufacturing), the PLAT (for service sector firms), and the PLAR (for research activities). The PAT also contains special provisions for projects undertaken by manufacturing firms in areas with serious unemployment problems due to industrial restructuring. Most PAT awards are job-related and in the maximum rate areas up to 50,000 francs is available per job created. In the standard award zones the maximum award is 35,000 francs per job created. For most manufacturing projects, awards also must remain under a ceiling expressed as a percentage of eligible project investment—25% in the maximum rate zone and 17% in the standard award zone. If projects are initiated in regions of very severe unemployment due to industrial restructuring, the job-related ceiling is waived completely and an additional subordinated loan is available.

A second important regional incentive is the regional employment grant (prime regionale a l'emploi, PRE). It is also a project-related grant available for the first 30 jobs created (or sometimes, maintained) within a firm. It is really a form of assistance to small firms throughout the country but its awards favor rural, remote, and mountainous areas. The standard award limit is 20,000 francs per job, but this is reduced to 10,000 francs in towns with a population greater than 100,000 and raised to 40,000 francs in areas handicapped by either demography or geography.

The third form of aid, the local business tax concession (exoneration de la taxe professionelle), at the maximum end exempts a firm from local business taxes for five years.[10] However, such taxes vary appreciably over the country so a percentage figure alone may be misleading. These regional incentives in France place far greater emphasis on jobs created than those in other European states. On the other hand, the level of incentive expenditures is rather low relative to other European programs which is somewhat surprising given the emphasis placed on regional development in France.

Early in 1984, the French government introduced an ambitious new package of regional development incentives focusing on what are called "Conversion Poles." Apparently different from the programs described above, it subsidizes new firms, attempts to influence wage schedules, and provides technical training. It operates in 15 areas of the country suffering particularly from the decline in steel, shipbuilding and coal. The program is designed to ameliorate the condition of life, improve the road system, construct new housing, and clean up industrial wastes. The cost of such activities is estimated at 1.1 billion francs. About 500 million francs have been allocated to the reorganization and improvement of educational and research institutions. A new National Institute of Technology is to be built near Creusot and several other research and technical centers are under consideration.

While it is probably too early to evaluate the program's success or failure, it was described with some skepticism in a recent newspaper story.[11] A major criticism focused on the overlapping activities of the many different state and local agencies involved which make program coordination difficult. The program has also been criticized for omitting several areas with even higher unemployment rates.

French regional policy not only attempts to channel employment and economic activity to depressed regions but also tries to prevent expansion in regions viewed as overdeveloped. Thus, an executive of a major aerospace firm noted that if his company wished to expand employment in Paris, it would first have to receive permission from the relevant authorities.

An electronics executive, while conceding the usefulness of government subsidies to cover the cost of training workers and building new factories in a designated "pole" area, complained that the government obliges firms to take questionable actions. He gave the example of government discouragement of plant closure and relocation, noting that it is often easier to close an outmoded plant and increase employment by expanding more attractive facilities elsewhere. The government had pressed firms to keep factories in the same place and to convert existing facilities rather than to move them.

Export Promotion and Financing

While most European countries have historically been much more dependent on foreign trade than the United States, French industrial policy appears to stress it more than the rest. Here, for example, is a French government official's description of how exports aided the development of the aerospace industry:

> In order to extend the scale of operations and to reduce average production costs, the national policy was then completed by an export promotion policy, which was particularly active during the 70s. Thanks to export credits and the effort of government diplomacy, the French aircraft industry was able to develop its sales in the Middle East (Saudi Arabia, Iraq, etc.), as well as in Latin America, Asian and African countries. Successful generations of missiles (Roland, Exocet, etc.) and of helicopters (Alouette) were developed for national needs and then exported by the same means.[12]

While it may be apocryphal, some have even suggested that export attractiveness may play a larger role in weapons development than the needs of the French armed forces. The statement of a French aerospace executive that "product development is a function of the export rate" and an electronics industry manager's blunt observation that "If we didn't sell abroad we couldn't survive," give some credence to that idea.

The importance of exports to the French arms industry is also stressed by government spokesmen. A high-ranking government official noted that shortly after the last socialist government took office there was some consideration given to restricting arms exports on political grounds but the idea was dropped after the "realities" were understood. These include the role of military exports in maintaining the state of the art and in preventing unemployment. The prevention of job loss operates both directly, in providing larger demand for labor, and indirectly, by constituting a filler for periods of reduced domestic arms purchases.

Two financial organizations facilitate French exports: the Banque Francaise du Commerce Exterieur (BFCE), and the Compagnie Francaise d'Assurance au Commerce Exterieur (COFACE). The former was established in 1946 to underwrite loans to finance manufacturing goods for export. Short and medium-term credits are provided for working capital and large orders. Special long-term loans with very low interest rates are also available. Short-term credits have been most utilized to finance exports of the automobile and vehicles, general machinery and electrical machinery industries. Substantial medium and long-term credits have also gone to the miscellaneous metal manufacturing, aircraft, and shipbuilding industries. COFACE guarantees exporters and investors against losses on their operations in foreign markets. Risks arising from manufacturing problems, political upheavals, credit failure, and natural catastrophies are covered.

Collaboration on projects with partners in other nations provides many of the advantages of exports—larger product runs and the ensuing scale economies. A government official, in supporting such projects, noted that in addition to reducing costs they provide protection from US competitors and add stability since they are more difficult to cancel than purely national projects.

Aerospatiale considers its partnership in civil aircraft (Airbus, etc.) and in tactical missiles with Messerschmitt-Bölkow-Blohm of West Germany in Euro-missile very important. An Aerospatiale executive noted that collaboration was the only way in which European firms can be strong enough to deal with American industry on an equal basis. He contrasted small European production of civil aircraft (280 by Fokker, and 250 Tridents and 100 BAC 111s by British Aerospace) with 1500 Boeing 727s and about the same number of 737s. The Airbus consortium members hope to produce approximately 1000 aircraft which would put them in a class with the US producers.[13]

Science and Technology Policies

The advance of science and technology has long been an important goal of the French government. During the 1970s emphasis was shifted from the support of R&D and prototype construction of particular products (Concorde, Airbus, etc.) to directing R&D funds to a broader front. Thus, six crucial areas were selected for support: bioengineering, marine industries, robotics, electronic office equipment, consumer electronics, and alternative energy technologies. The recent Socialist government expanded efforts to improve the competitiveness of French industry via the promotion of scientific research and innovation.

There has been a rapid series of changes in the French government structure responsible for the administration of science and technology. Thus, in 1981–1982 the Ministries of Research and of Industry were merged into a "super ministry" with a substantial budget to expand R&D activities. After a brief period, there was another change which reconstituted the two separate ministries—a Ministry of Research and Technology and a Ministry of Industrial Redeployment and External Trade.

The Ministry of Research and Technology was organized into several divisions, one of which was charged with functions similar to those of the predecessor Delegation Generale a la Recherche Scientifique et Technique (DGRST). This group, which apparently no longer has a separate existence, played an important coordinating role in preparing the annual civilian science budget.[14] Another reorganization was under consideration during the last days of the recent Socialist regime, indicating the state of flux in the government administration for science.[15] Regardless of the final organization that emerges, it appears that a recent and potentially important function will remain: the coordination of activities in industry and various research organizations in order to bridge gaps between the researchers and to focus on a common objective.[16] Several so-called Programmes Mobilisateurs had been established to carry out this mission in several crucial sectors.

The Technological R&D Orientation Act of June 1982 set annual increases in budget appropriations for research at near 18% until 1985 as part of an effort to bring R&D activities to 2.5% of the GNP by 1985.[17] In addition, the Act provided for cooperation betwen public and private industries on innovation projects. The 1983 Finance Act also provided a tax credit equal to 25% of the increase in the R&D expenditures of a company.

The detailed budget figures for 1987 released in Paris in October 1986 call for an overall planned increase of 8.1% in government-funded R&D over 1986 with larger relative gains for basic research and for military R&D. While the planned volume of government-funded civil R&D is to fall by 2.3% from the 1985 level, the last full year in power of the socialist regime, the R&D budget will increase from 7.2% to 7.6% of aggregate public spending. Indirect support for research continues via increased tax credits to industry. Despite conservative advocacy of a reduced government role, the new minister for Research and Higher Education, Alain Devaquet, recently observed that the need of France "is not for less, or more, but *better* state [control]."[18] In line with this view, Devaquet revealed several proposals designed to improve the operations of the Centre Nationale de la Recherche Scientifique (CNRS), the main government sponsored research agency.[19]

Of particular interest for moving new ideas into industry is the Agence Nationale De Valorisation De la Recherche (ANVAR).[20] The organization has three essential missions:

- to serve as a consultant to those interested in developing inventions;
- to develop innovations both in firms (of all sizes) and public laboratories;
- to help investment based on technology in firms.

In 1979, the organization was regionalized and it now operates in 24 regions of the country. Each regional director is authorized to make his own decision on financial aid grants of up to 1 million francs for development and up to 5 million francs for technology-based investment. ANVAR was formed in 1968 and one of its principal tasks was to encourage and speed the diffusion of knowledge into industry. This is still true but current ANVAR procedure is to operate in a consultative role. It is also able to put funds into development as an interest-free loan. Given its functions, ANVAR is close to both the banking system and the research community. Recent reorganization of government ministries was designed to create a network of partners among the different ministries to encourage and speed up promising research. The goal now is to have someone in each French public organization responsible for the spread of innovation. This includes defense laboratories as well as civilian institutions.

In recent years ANVAR has grown both in staff and in budget, and is now prepared to play a central role.[21] It no longer focuses its activities on the smaller or medium-sized enterprises. Its staff has grown from about 100 persons in 1979 and is expected soon to reach 450. As French firms become more involved in international markets they will need asistance with patents, marketing, product design, financing etc., and ANVAR is attempting to provide consultant services for these functions. A relatively new ANVAR function is to interest young people in science and technology, and this function has attracted much foreign interest, particularly from the Dutch and the Swedes.

Also of interest was the comment of an ANVAR official that his organization does not distinguish between firms on the basis of the citizenship of the owners. Thus, ANVAR has, in several cases, worked with US firms which will develop technology discovered in French laboratories. Presumably production will take place both in the US and in France.

Filiere Electronique

A major endeavor of the Socialist government had been the promotion of the filieres concept which focuses on coordinating the activities of industrial sectors along the lines of their vertical structuring—all the way from raw materials to final market. The Filiere Electronique had received the most attention and will be described briefly. Basically, it stressed the technological interdependence between the various industrial sectors which incorporate electronic technologies.

Analysis of the French electronics industry indicated the coexistence of strong points and weak ones. Positions of strength were found in professional electronic equipment and telecommunications. Average performance was the rule in computers and electronic components, while electronic consumer goods, office equipment, robotics, and scientific instruments appeared to be lagging. The key element of the strategy was to improve the weak areas of the industry by reliance upon the strong ones.

Principal emphasis was planned for integrated circuits, computers, electronic consumer goods, and robots. The goal was to devote approximately 140 billion (1982) francs to R&D and investment over the 1984–1987 period with the objective of attaining an annual growth rate of 9% and a trade surplus of 20 billion francs by 1987. This compares with 1981 figures of 3% and a trade deficit of 10 billion francs. The electronics firms themselves, were to finance the effort, with government aid originally scheduled from the Ministries of Defense, PTT, and Industry and Research. Implementation of the plan was the responsibility of the four major electronics firms (then all nationalized): Thomson, CIT-Alcatel, Matra, and Bull. These four firms have all been subjected to a process of restructuring to reduce overlapping of specializations.

French public procurement has played a major role in strengthening professional electronic equipment. Here the main firms are Thomson-CSF, a subsidiary of the Thomson conglomerate organization, and Matra. In telecommunications Thomson-CSF is found again, as is CIT-Alcatel, a subsidiary of the Group Compagnie Generale d'Electricite (CGE).

Since the early 1950s a policy of self-reliance in electronic equipment has been followed by the Defense Ministry and the National Broadcasting Authority. French firms received research contracts from the MOD to develop radar, aircraft equipment, and missiles. Their production was facilitated by long-term contracts. Ultimate scale economies were attained and R&D spending was amortized through an extensive export program aided by loans and the efforts of French diplomatic representatives abroad.

For years France has relied upon such telecommunications giants as ITT and Ericsson. In the late 1960s the PTT's research unit, Centre National d'Etudes des Telecommunications (CNET), scored some important breakthroughs and transferred the technology to CIT-Alcatel. Substantial public investment in telecommunications equipment was undertaken by the French government in the early 1970s. Later, as part of the nationalization program, ITT-France and Ericsson France were merged into Thomson-CSF. The telecommunications industry was transformed as a result of public procurement (30 billion francs [1983] annually over the past decade) and large research support.[22] R&D programs are under way in fibre optics, computers, and domestic terminals.

Less success has been attained in electronic components and computers. French efforts in computer technology have continued for some time. Thus, Plan Calcul was begun in 1966 as one of the major Gaullist projects aimed at national self-sufficiency. As the private French computer firm, Bull, had been bought by General Electric of the US a few years earlier, a semipublic company, CII, was funded jointly with cooperation from Thomson and CGE. The Industry Ministry monitored government research grants and public procurement. In 1975 CII merged with Bull which then had become part of Honeywell of the US. The new firm became CII-Honeywell Bull (CII-HB) and is now the largest European computer firm. However, despite subsidies and public procurement, the company still experiences losses and bears substantial debt. In 1982 government support to CII-HB was increased, and two other French firms in minicomputers and peripherals, SEMS and Transac, were merged into CII-HB to form Groupe Bull, which focuses on the next generation of computers.

In early December 1986 a restructuring of Honeywell's computer operations was announced. Under the new arrangement a consortium will be established in which Groupe Bull and NEC of Japan will share in Honeywell's computer business. Initially these two organizations will have respectively, 42.5% and 15% shares, while Honeywell retains 42.5%. The terms of the agreement permit Honeywell to reduce its equity to 19.9% in two years while only Bull can increase its holdings to 65.1%. Honeywell has made clear its intention to sharply contract its non-governmental computer activities so Bull will control the board.[23]

The integrated circuit plan was initiated in 1976 with five firms receiving research grants from the Ministry of Industry and orders from the Ministries of Defense and PTT to develop LSI circuits. The government also encouraged them to enter into agreements with leading US firms in the hope that this would lead to successful technology transfer. In 1982, public support increased and the electronic components sector reorganized around Thomson and Matra.

Recently, two weak sectors of the electronics industry which had been outside the plan, consumer electronics and robotics, were incorporated into the plan filiere electronique. Thomson was encouraged to expand its consumer electronics efforts in the European market and acquired AEG-Telefunken in West Germany. French cooperative efforts (via Thomson) with the Japanese group Matsushita-JVC in the production of video tape recorders are also being urged.

A restructuring of the French machine tool industry was begun in 1981 to improve its capabilities in robotics. Smaller firms have been encouraged to merge and enhance their capabilities in numerically-controlled machine tools and related equipment. The *quid pro quo* is to consist of a package of research grants, purchases by the nationalized firms and training programs, with monitoring by the Industry Ministry.

Other Major Industrial Policy Ventures

French industrial policy initiatives have been largely successful in energy and aerospace, with national independence largely attained in each. In the energy area, state regulation of oil and gas imports was authorized by a 1928 law. An independent French oil industry was established in the 1960s when the two government-controlled firms, Total-Compagnie Francaise des Petroles and Elf-Aquitaine together accounted for 50% of the national oil market. With government aid they have built an advanced industry in refining, petrochemicals, and oil-related services.

State monopolies in coal, gas and electricity have dominated the energy sector since the 1946 nationalizations. Charbonnages de France, Gaz de France and Electricite de France are all familiar names in their respective markets.

The French Atomic Energy Commission (Commissariat a l'Energie Atomique, CEA) was established in 1945. It conducted both basic and military research. French holdings of uranium mines were expanded in the 1960s when the national nuclear force was established and a militarily-oriented uranium enrichment plant was built in the southeast region at Pierrelatte. Early efforts to develop electric generating reactors using the graphite-carbon dioxide method failed, and consequently, the government obtained licensing rights from Westinghouse to build a pressurized water reactor facility, and a low-enrichment uranium plant was built at Tricastin. The enrichment facility has Italian, Spanish, and several other foreign partners and is known as Eurodif.

French nuclear boilers are fabricated by Framatome, a subsidiary of the CEA and the private engineering group, Schneider. Originally a licensee of Westinghouse, Framatome become independent in 1980. Alsthom, a subsidiary of the nationalized group CGE, builds the electric generators. French nuclear efforts were rounded out by an expansion of the Eurodif enrichment plant, the construction of a plant to reprocess spent nuclear fuel at La Hague in the west, and pilot research on a fast breeder-reactor known as Superphenix. French capabilities over the entire nuclear cycle are now conceded to be excellent.

The nuclear electricity-generating program was reduced somewhat in 1981. The planned annual addition of six 900-megawatt plants has been reduced to two or three-1300 megawatt plants. Nuclear generated electricity now represents close to half of the total electricity usage in France and the 1990 goal is 75%. By then oil's share of energy generation will have fallen to a third, down from 60% in 1973.

It is interesting to note that as the domestic nuclear equipment market shrunk in recent years the industry heavily expanded its efforts in developing export markets. There is every reason to expect a similar reaction to any sizable cuts in arms procurement by the French armed forces. It is a predictable natural reaction.

To round out the energy picture it should be noted that significant government programs have also been started to develop energy conservation and such new energy sources as solar photovoltaic cells, geothermy, and biomass. The government monitors were the Ministry of Industry and Research (while still unified) and the subsidiary Agence Francaise pour la Maitrise de l'Energie.

French successes in aerospace are unquestioned. After many mergers and corporate restructurings, three principal firms account for the bulk of the industry's output: Societe Nationale Industrielle Aerospatiale (SNIAS), which focuses on civil passenger aircraft, helicopters, missiles, space launchers, and satellites; Dassault-Breguet in military aircraft; and Societe Nationale D'Etude et De Construction De Moteurs D'Aviation (SNECMA) in aeroengines. Several smaller firms have carved out an important niche for themselves in specialized areas such as Matra in missiles and Turbomeca in helicopter engines.

With national independence as the principal goal, public procurement, research subsidies and export credits have been the natural instruments. A highly successful family of military aircraft has been developed over the years at Avions Marcel Dassault, recently merged with Breguet-Aviation. Dassault's legendary success at producing technically excellent aircraft that are relatively inexpensive, and relatively simple to operate and maintain, has made it a subject of inquiry for US scholars.[24] A very important point here is whether the successes of Dassault can reasonably be attributed to French industrial policy. While undoubtedly benefiting from public procurement and export promotion efforts, Dassault's successes were attained while it operated as an essentially private firm. The founder of the firm, Marcel Dassault (recently deceased), and his designers are clearly unique and not easily duplicated. The firm was one of those nationalized in the 1981 wave.

French aerospace technology has been transferred to non-military uses, both in civil aircraft and space ventures. The Caravelle and Concorde were both technical successes but commercial disappointments. France, via Aerospatiale and SNECMA, plays a leading role in the European Airbus project, but it is too early to evaluate its success or failure (see Note 13). It is heavily subsidized by its cooperating member states which now also include the Federal Republic of Germany, the United Kingdom, and Spain.

France has been active in space activities for some time. Its space agency, the Centre National d'Etudes Spatiales (CNES) traces back to the Gaullist period. The launching base at Kourou in French Guyana has been active in both French and European space efforts. While CNES has participated in French military projects, its civil activities are now conducted with other members of the European Space Agency. Commercial space efforts such as the launcher Ariane are now conducted within the consortium known as Arianespace.

Evaluation of French Industrial Policy

Electronics, energy, and aerospace represent areas where the French goals of attaining technologically advanced capability levels and a competitive position on world markets have been realized. The record is more spotty in other target industries of French industrial policy such as advanced shipbuilding, railroad equipment, and pharmaceuticals. Such sectors as precision instruments, robotics, very-large-scale-integrated (VLSI) electronic components, coal liquefaction, biochemistry, and sophisticated machinery have turned in disappointing results.

These divergent achievements by sector challenge the investigator to find the common thread which differentiates the successes from the failures. In his interesting paper, Stoffaes singles out the nature of the market. Thus:

> A common characteristic of the sectors where French industry has reached a strong technological and commercial position is their high dependence on government procurement policy and state intervention. In advanced technologies, France seems to be good in sectors whose government administrations are the main customers, and not so good in sectors producing for mass consumption or for general industrial equipment. Still more significant . . . is that the main objective of these government industrial strategies seems to have been national security. . . . Even if those industrial policies subsequently produced applications in non-military areas, their origins can almost always be traced to national independence objectives.[25]

Against this background, it is interesting to note the French reaction to the US invitation that our European allies participate in the research program for the new Strategic Defense Initiative (SDI). The European governments initially appeared to grope for a response in an environment which appeared confused and characterized by many cross currents. Their hesitation reflected a variety of political and economic uncertainties.[26] In the midst of this confusion, France proposed an alternative route—European collaboration in a series of advanced technology research projects organized under the title "Eureka," (European Research Cooperation Agency). The French Minister for External Relations, Roland Dumas, originally wrote to his European counterparts proposing joint super computers; high-powered lasers and particle beams; artificial intelligence; and high-speed microelectronics. There is apparently a fair amount of overlapping between these fields and those to be studied under SDI,[27] but the French initially stressed peaceful uses ("Star Peace").[28] An important goal would be to help Europe catch up with the US and Japan in several critical technology areas.[29] In Dumas' words, ". . . if we do not quickly harmonize our policies, nothing can prevent our research workers, our capital, and our industrialists from giving in to the temptation of ad-hoc cooperation, with the role of Europe [in the SDI program] becoming reduced to that of a subcontractor."[30]

The rationale for Dumas' proposal reflects a familiar, but as yet, unsolved dilemma—namely, that the European community as a whole may have different interests than those in the individual firms.[31] Thus, individual European firms may find it more interesting to participate in joint ventures with American or Japanese firms because of the resulting access to more advanced technology and larger markets. However, if most European firms feel this way, it may be harmful to Europe as a whole if its firms become subcontractors due to weaknesses in European research and development and too narrow an array of products. It is also occasionally noted that the heightened US concern in recent years over technology loss to the Eastern Bloc has made it more difficult for European allies to gain access to US universities and laboratories. This provides an additional impetus for a more coordinated effort in research and science by the Europeans.

Despite the theoretical appeal of such a coordinated effort, many European firms have become impatient at the prospect of sacrificing the good for the perfect and have pressed for a role in both the Eureka and SDI programs. Thus, while among the European states, only the UK, the Federal Republic of Germany, and Italy have negotiated formal memoranda of understanding with the US on participation in SDI, many advanced technology firms in other European countries are competing for SDI contracts, in some cases with their government's blessing.

Indeed, in late 1986 the US Strategic Defense Initiative Organization selected seven multinational consortia to receive contracts for Phase I studies of the architecture of a European defense against tactical missiles. The contracts covered 29 firms in six European countries (the UK, West Germany, Italy, France, the Netherlands, and Belgium). The total value of the seven contracts was $14 million but the successful teams will be in a position to compete for much larger contracts for further stages in a multibillion-dollar European theater missile defense program.[32] A growing awareness of the complementarity between research on defense against missiles of various ranges has led to close contact between the US SDI and NATO studies of a new antitactical missile system. Among the goals are utilization of applicable technology and the avoidance of duplication.[33] Another indication of changing attitudes was the dispatch of a high level delegation from the French Delegation General Pour l'Armament (DGA) to the US for discussion of a potential French role in the SDI program.[34]

Nevertheless, Eureka appears to have moved ahead with surprising speed and most reports of the third ministerial conference held in London in the early summer of 1986 have reflected optimism.[35] A total of sixty-two projects worth more than $2 billion were approved at the meeting attended by ministers from nineteen countries. These projects are in addition to ten original projects approved at a November 1985 conference.

In mid-December of 1986 a new group of thirty-seven corporate research ventures were approved under the Eureka program at a meeting in Stockholm. However, it is important to recognize that the mere designation of a project as a Eureka venture essentially consists of a gesture of approval which endorses it as a worthwhile idea deserving of financial support. That support, however, is expected to come from each government, acting on its own in determining the level of actual support it will contribute. This vagueness of funding together with a loose organization which lacks a central authority to check on the progress of individual projects has contributed to some skepticism among European firms concerning the potential value of the Eureka program.[36]

This section might appropriately be concluded with a summary of a recent OECD assessment of French innovation policy. After praising the increase in R&D spending from 1.8% to 2.25% of GNP over the life of the last socialist regime and the success of several of the *grandes programmes* the report criticizes the French fascination with *grandeur* which often is accompanied with a bureaucratic elitism damaging to innovation and enterprise. To counter such problems the report's authors recommend that France:

- aim at educating 80% of the population to the level of *baccalaureat* and reduce some of the barriers between the grandes écoles and less prestigious educational establishments;
- encourage joint ventures between engineering and basic-research centers and more exchanges between industry, the universities, and the government-sponsored Centre National de la Recherche Scientifique;
- continue the decentralization of government functions away from Paris— particularly those concerned with incentives and small business;
- expand its involvement in European projects such as Ariane and Airbus but focus more on smaller projects.[37]

Dependence on the Military Customer

Table 3.1 summarizes several aspects of military-industrial relationships in France with the value of arms sales and the percentage of those sales exported by major firms shown in the upper panel of the table.

Personal interviews yielded additional information on military dependence. An executive at Aerospatiale noted that in terms of both sales and employment, the military share varies substantially between divisions. The ballistic missile division works only for the government with the military accounting for 75% of employment and civilian space activities accounting for the rest. Essentially, all employment in the tactical missile division is devoted to the military. The division of employment in helicopter production is approximately 50-50.

On civil aircraft development, mainly the airbus and the joint Franco-Italian ATR 42, the company has provided substantial development funds and has received loans from the government. The Transall military transport is close to the end of production and is not an important project now. The Epsilon beginning trainer is figured as four-fifths civil.

In general, at the start of a military project the government pays the costs. However, when it comes to exports, the company's own money is at risk. Ballistic missiles for the military and for space launcher use are not exported. While Aerospatiale does not develop military aircraft, it often functions as a subcontractor of Dassault, usually working on the wings. There is no competition between the two firms.

Aerospatiale employs a total of 40,000 persons, about a fifth of whom work in Paris. It also operates a US subsidiary located in Grand Prairie, Texas, near Dallas, which focuses on helicopters. About 100 of these helicopters have been sold to the US Coast Guard.

An executive of the electronics firm, Thomson CSF, noted that his firm tries to be prepared for changes in domestic military expenditures but that the major risk is found in export markets which tend to be more unstable. The company attempts to limit its backlog of sales to the French government to under 40% and to avoid allowing its sales to any foreign country to exceed 15% of the total. He conceded that sales to Saudi Arabia do, in fact, exceed this limit, but emphasized that in the long term it is important for the company to avoid overdependence on any single customer. About one-third of sales are destined for the military.

A special assistant in the cabinet of the Minister of Industrial Redeployment and Foreign Trade observed that a company like Thomson couldn't be efficient in the military market if it was not efficient in other markets since the military market did not provide sufficient opportunities for the firm's complete development of a full range of products. Thus, the government encouraged careful diversification activities among its military suppliers. An increased civil market share also is viewed as a means to enhance technology transfer. A French banker noted another link between the military and civil sides—the important cash flow made available to firms to use for civil development which results from the fact that they are so well paid by the government for their military work.

Transferability Between Military and Civil Divisions

Employees occasionally transfer between divisions of Aerospatiale, but it is infrequent. Apparently it is easier to transfer executives than assembly line workers. Obviously there is a great deal of variation between products. In some cases a product is classified as military only because of the identity of the buyer. This is particularly so in the case of avionics and radar.

Thomson's policy is to mix military and civil products in the same division and occasionally even in the same plant, but that is apparently more difficult. If for no other reason, considerations of security may inhibit production at a common site. Different objectives also tend to discourage common production. Thus, an electronics industry official emphasized that price considerations are more important in civil markets subject to greater competition while performance objectives seem to dominate military production with price being somewhat less important. It was stressed that while the company will fill its commitments to the letter in both type markets, it must always be ready to change military specifications with little notice. This means that military products tend to be more customized and less like standard items which can sit as inventory on-the-shelf for some extended period.

There has been some transfer of manpower at Thomson. Some 1200 employees at the Laval plant who once produced telephones have been shifted to military radio communications. Five Thomson plants have experienced this type of change in these last five years as the PTT drastically increased its orders of digital equipment. Productivity has increased much faster in telecommunications than in military equipment or in medical and consumer goods products. The increase experienced in foreign military sales has provided a means to attain employment stability, an important goal in France. The military work has been used as a filler. Thus, the problem has been to adjust to a civil to military transfer of resources. While the work still involves electronics, the company estimates that about one year is necessary to train and adjust workers who are being transferred from civil to military work.

Climate Required for Ease of Adjustment and Innovation

A successful policy requires not only well-designed mechanisms or instruments but also an environment which encourages their intelligent application. Two thoughtful observers of the French scene, a banker and an economist, commented at length on the environment for change and innovation in France. Both identified powerful structural obstacles to the attainment of the goals of French industrial policy.[38]

The banker contrasted the different experiences of France and the United States in utilizing pubic funds to aid the general economy. The banker saw the US as the more successful in utilizing the defense and space budgets to strengthen the capacity and power of its industry. He saw the basic problem in France to be the focus on large firms and the failure to develop an extensive system of subcontracting which would "irrigate small business," as well as large. In his opinion large firms were not where imagination and innovation occur most often. He also saw ANVAR's recent actions in intensively funding large firms as an error if they are in fact desirous of encouraging high technology. Funneling savings to ANVAR for distribution to industry will therefore not help alleviate the venture capital scarcity which troubles small and medium-sized French firms. The talk of supporting innovation and moving ideas more rapidly from invention to utilization is, he feared, just fashionable talk without much in the way of results because of the continuing focus on large firms.

He also called attention to the French "caste system" which discourages the appearance of "self-made men" who are more likely to be innovative in their approach to problems. Specifically, he identified the great similarity in educational background of the leaders of France (political, military, and industrial). The overwhelming number of the French elite are graduates of the École Polytechnique and the École Nationale d'Administration. While people of working class background are occasionally admitted (more frequently to the Polytechnique than to ENA), they were described as "more molded by it than modifying it." Thus, a common approach to problem-solving emerges which pervades the executive suites of most French institutions. Not only do the graduates of these Grandes Écoles think the same way, but they naturally favor one another—making it very difficult for the "self-made man" to advance. My respondent saw this as inhibiting major breakthroughs which one might otherwise expect from such a highly educated and well-trained population. As he put it, "most French civil servants in 1970 were still trying do what Mussolini did in Italy in the 1930s."

My economist respondent cited results of a survey by Elf-Aquitaine on venture capital use in France to support good ideas during a recent three-year period. Of each 100 francs expended, 90 would be spent in the US, 5 in West Germany, 2 in Japan, and 3 in France. In his judgment this allocation reflected the differential climate for innovation in these four countries. He stressed that the scarcity in France was not of good ideas or able people, but rather of an environment in which their promise could be realized.

He saw the recent moves in France in the direction of deregulation of industry and the apparent willingness to accept bankruptcies in older basic industries, despite the resulting unemployment, as positive signs. The virtue of flexibility is now being recognized and he was hopeful that good results could be realized if this was joined to a move to reduce protectionism. In the past, public sector purchases have been the last stronghold of the buy-national preference, and a real common market in these areas could bring excellent results. In addition to the defense market, he also saw the area of health-related equipment as quite promising. In his opinion, a "Europe of projects," that is, strong joint ventures without specific state intervention would be an important step forward. He also emphasized that the US should not be reluctant to see, and even help, the Europeans to grow stronger since it was also helping itself by doing so because it was important to have strong, reliable friends.

Summary

Of the major countries visited, France has the oldest traditions of government intervention and the least reluctance to use it in the name of national interest. There are no shortages of areas in which French excellence is evident, but it is less obvious that these successes can be attributed to industrial policy. As noted above, there is good reason to credit public procurement in those industries and sectors where the best results have been attained. National security has also been closely related to the activities of these industries. Thus, of all the activities of the French government to aid strategic sectors, the most important may have been to provide markets. In the final analysis, all the other measures will be wasted if a useful product does not emerge. This point was well-illustrated by a remark of a high ranking executive of a major French firm which can be identified as a "national champion." After reviewing the entire array of national-industrial policies he concluded "we would prefer to have orders and do things ourselves."

A foreign observer also would be tempted to attribute the successes of Dassault, for example, to an uncommon mixture of inspired talent and hard work in an environment which appreciated and rewarded these qualities and which minimized bureaucratic interventions. Its extensive activities abroad also threw it into a competitive environment which it lacked at home and from which it may have benefited. The otherwise absence of competition faced by a national champion may inhibit its development.

The criticism of the influence of a very small number of schools which, however excellent academically, apparently narrowly channel the thinking of their graduates is difficult for an outsider to evaluate. The old school tie phenomenon is not unknown in the United States, but there are a substantially larger number of excellent universities. While a number of French graduates of the Grandes Ecoles acquire masters' degrees at top American universities, it may be difficult for them to start their own businesses when they return home. In an environment which discourages risk taking, it may be easier and safer simply to join a large established French firm. If the current educational system does contribute to this pernicious influence, some changes might be in order. A review of French educational policy is now under way but, thus far, it has been limited to public education at the primary school level.[39]

In view of the heavy emphasis already devoted to export markets as a complement to domestic arms sales, a substantial reduction in purchases by the French Armed Forces would likely be accompanied by an even heavier emphasis on foreign sales. One can easily envision a substantial intensification of competition in export markets. Should that avenue of adjustment be reduced by restrictions on military exports the pressure to find alternative products would be intense and some efforts in that direction would probably be prudent.

Notes

1. Christian Stoffaes, "Industrial Policy in High Technology Industries: The French Experience," unpublished paper presented at Brookings Institution Conference on Industrial Policy in France and its implications for the United States, September 27–28, 1984, pp. 5–6. Much of the following historical summary is taken from this source.

2. Stoffaes, "Industrial Policy in High Technology Industries: The French Experience," p. 6.

3. This section is based, in part, on Suomela, *et al.*, US International Trade Commission, Foreign Industrial Targeting and Its Effect on US Industries, Phase II:, pp. 44–67; and Franko, *European Industrial Policy: Past, Present, and Future*, pp. 15–16, 25–29, and 58–59.

4. Suomela, *et al.*, US International Trade Commission, Foreign Industrial Targeting and Its Effect on US Industries, Phase II:, p. 45.

5. Some movement toward denationalization may be anticipated after the conservative electoral victory in the spring of 1986.

6. Much of this section borrows from Christian Stoffaes, "Industrial Policy in High Technology Industries: The French Experience."

7. The newly-elected conservative government has abolished the Ministry of Research and Technology in the latest of a series of structural reorganizations of the science administrative mechanism. Responsibility for research is now divided between the Ministries of Industry and Education. At this time, it is unclear where the coordinative function is to be lodged. For speculation on the administrative control of French science policy see: "French Laboratories—Scientists Take to the Barricades," *The Economist*, July 26, 1986, p. 82; and "French Science Policy Breaking 300-Year Mold," *Science*, March 7, 1986, pp. 1060–1062.

8. Stoffaes, "Industrial Policy in High Technology Industries: The French Experience," p.12. This is, indeed, a unique French phenomenon and more will be said below about its possible impact on the French economy's ability to adapt to rapidly changing circumstances such as a sharp reduction in military expenditures.

9. This section borrows from Yuill & Allen, *European Regional Incentives, 1984*, pp. 45–46, and 179–216.

10. This advantage is somewhat reduced, however, by a recent change which provides that firms established in 1983 or 1984, or which took over a company in difficulty during that period, may receive a total exemption from local business tax and property tax for two years regardless of location. See Yuill & Allen, *European Regional Incentives*, p. 45.

11. "Les Poles de Conversion Ont Un An," *Le Monde*, February 5, 1985, p. 23.

12. Stoffaes, "Industrial Policy in High Technology Industries: The French Experience," p. 21.

13. For recent views on Airbus' chances for success, see: "Airbus Industrie Officials Confident on Obtaining Funding for A330/A340," *Aviation Week and Space Technology*, June 16, 1986, p. 49; and "Airbus Shows How It Will Take on Boeing in the Battle for the Skies," *Die Zeit*, Hamburg, May 30, 1986, translated in *The German Tribune: A Weekly Review of the German Press*, June 15, 1986, p. 9. For a thoughtful negative opinion see "Europe's Dream Machines," *The Economist*, January 25, 1986, pp. 14–15.

14. See Udis, *From Guns to Butter*, pp. 85–86 for a description of the functions and operations of DGRST.

15. See "French Science Policy Breaking 300-Year Mold," pp. 1060–1062.

16. See "French Science Policy Breaking 300-Year Mold," p. 1061.

17. While this goal was not attained, government spending on R&D rose on the average by more than 7% a year in the 1981–1985 period during which several thousand new scientific posts were created in government laboratories. See "French Laboratories: Scientists Take to the Barricades."

18. See "French R&D: á la Reagan with Dash of DeGaulle," *Science*, October 24, 1986, pp. 417–418.

19. See "French R&D: á la Reagan with Dash of DeGaulle," *Science*, October 24, 1986, pp. 417–418.

20. For an earlier description of ANVAR see Udis, *From Guns to Butter*, pp. 91–93.

21. The new conservative government may change this and recent reports indicate a sharp cut in ANVAR's budget. See "Research Fares Well in New French Budget," *Science*, August 15, 1986, p. 718.

22. The most recent development in telecommunications is the sale to state-owned Compagnie Générale d'Electricité (CGE) of close to 60% of the continental European telecommunications assets of International Telephone and Telegraph (ITT) of the United States. See "ITT: Phone Company Without a Line," *The Economist*, July 5, 1986 pp. 59–60 and "Behind the ITT Deal: Will Araskog's Radical Surgery Work?" *Business Week*, July 14, 1986, pp. 62–64. See also "CGE Pact Won't Include ITT Holding in a British Cable Maker, STC-PLC," *Wall Street Journal*, December 31, 1986, p. 4. The plan became enmeshed in a highly complex and bitter competition between AT&T of the US and British, West German, and Swedish firms to become the second source of telephone switching equipment to the French government. See "French Telecommunications Plans Snarled," *Wall Street Journal*, October 15, 1986, p. 36; "Europe Tries to Break Up AT&T's Affair with France," *Business Week*, November 3, 1986, p. 49; "European Telecommunications: The High-Wire Act Over CGCT,"

The Economist, November 6, 1986, pp. 81–82; "France Will Limit Foreign Ownership In Telecommunications Firm to 20%," *Wall Street Journal,* December 2, 1986, p. 40; "FCC in a Trade Move Proposes to Block Phone Gear Sales by Some Foreign Firms," *Wall Street Journal,* December 24, 1986, p. 32. By year end 1986, a formal CGE-ITT agreement was expected to be signed under the terms of which CGE and ITT were to merge their telecommunications and some fiber-optics cable activities in the new venture to be incorporated in the Netherlands. CGE will own between 51% and 59% of the new company, depending on its final configuration, Credit Lyonnais of France will own about 2%, Societe Generale de Belgique, a Belgian banking group will hold 6%. ITT would retain a share between 35% and 37%. See "Formal CGE-ITT Accord Is Seen Today for Giant Telecommunications Venture," *Wall Street Journal,* December 30, 1986, p. 6. A very interesting perspective is presented in "CGE Plans to Savage ITT In Order to Save It," *Business Week,* December 29, 1986, p. 49. The circumstances leading to the transaction are detailed as a case study of current conditions in the international telecommunications industry in "Telephone Switch: ITT-CGE Deal shows the Change Buffetting Telecommunications," *Wall Street Journal,* April 30, 1987, p. 1.

23. See "Honeywell Beats a Retreat From the Computer Wars," *Business Week,* December 15, 1986, p. 30. However, some observers have questioned the stability of such an operation since Japan's NEC is viewed as the strongest partner, technologically and financially. See for example, "Honeywell May Get a Boss, Not A Partner, In NEC," *Business Week,* October 20, 1986, pp. 43–46.

24. See, for example, Robert Perry, *A Dassault Dossier: Aircraft Acquisition in France,* (Santa Monica, California: the Rand Corporation, R-1148-PR, September 1973); and Edgar E. Ulsamer, "The Designers of Dassault: Men Who Take One Step At A Time," *Air Force Magazine,* Vol. 32 (August 1970).

25. Stoffaes, "Industrial Policy in High Technology Industries: The French Experience," p. 15.

26. See "Manna from Heaven," *The Economist,* April 27, 1985, pp. 18–19.

27. Some specific examples of such overlapping between SDI and Eureka may be found in "European Industry Begins to Seek U.S. SDI Contracts," *Aviation Week and Space Technology,* December 16, 1985, pp. 12–15.

28. Not all Europeans are happy with the ostensibly peaceful orientation of Eureka-sponsored research. At a conference in Paris in November 1986 Etienne Davignon, director of the Societe General de Belgique and a former vice president of the Commision of European Communities expressed the opinion that Europe missed "a great opportunity" when direct military programs were excluded from the Eureka program. See "SDIO to Examine Existing Allied Ballistic Missile Defense Systems," *Aviation Week and Space Technology,* November 24, 1986, pp. 26–27.

29. See "France Seeks Joint European Research," *Science,* May 10, 1985, p. 694.

30. See "France Seeks Joint European Research," *Science,* May 10, 1985, p. 694.

31. A similar dilemma exists which may pit the interests of individual nations against those of the European community as a whole. For a report which examines a growing rift between the "Big Three" (The United Kingdom, France, and West Germany) and the smaller EEC states over research funding, See "EEC Research: More Do-It-Yourself," *The Economist,* July 26, 1986, p. 46.

32. See "SDIO Selects Multinational Teams to Study European Missile Defense," *Aviation Week and Space Technology,* December 8, 1986, pp. 18–19.

33. See "NATO Accelerates Antitactical Missile Defense Research," *Aviation Week and Space Technology,* June 2, 1986, pp. 69–71.

34. See "French Signals," *Aviation Week and Space Technology,* November 3, 1986, p. 31.

35. See "Europeans Approve Projects for Eureka Worth $2 Billion," *Aviation Week and Space Technology*, July 7, 1986, p. 27; "Eureka!," p. 16 and "Eureka: Less Foggy," p. 75, *The Economist*, July 5, 1986; "The 19 Eureka Countries Try to Find It in London," *Der Tagesspiegel*, Berlin, July 1, 1986, translated in *The German Tribune*, July 13, 1986, pp. 2–3. An account which focuses more on potential problems is found in "Europe Pushes Ahead with Plans for Joint Projects," *Science*, July 11, 1986, p. 152.

36. See "EC Minsters Fail to Agree On Technology Subsidies," *Wall Street Journal*, December 18, 1986, p. 28. However, at the above mentioned Stockholm conference Britain's Minister of State for Industry and Information Technology, Geoffrey Pattie, spoke of a growing enthusiasm for Eureka resulting from two factors: projects are directly selected by the companies themselves, and emphasis is placed on "market-opening measures" such as promoting common standards. See "EEC Research Program in Jeopardy," *Science*, January 9, 1987, p. 158.

37. See "French Technology: Petit est Beau," *The Economist*, March 1, 1986, pp. 80–82.

38. These views are those of only two people, not the views of a scientifically selected sample. Their inclusion reflects my belief that they are thought-provoking, not necessarily that they are "correct."

39. See "French Education: Back to Basics," *Science*, March 15, 1985, p. 227.

54

TABLE 3.1 FRANCE: The Military Industrial Complex in High Technologies

Main Firms and Military Establishments

	Thomson CSF	Aero-spatiale	Dassault Breguet	Dion Tech des Construc. Navales (DTCN)	Commissariat a l'Energie Atomique (CEA)	Groupt. Industrial des Arme Terrestres (GIAT)	SNECMA	MATRA	Ste Nale des Poudres et Explosifs (SNPE)	MANU-RHIN
Arms sales billion francs)	14	11	10	10	6.5	6	3.5	3	1.2	1.1
of which exports (in %)	65	55	75	7	0	40	50	70	35	75

Military Research Expenditures

Share of Total Sales in Armament by Sector

Pourcentage du Chiffre D'Affaires total du secteur realise dans l'armement	Construction aeronautique	70%
	Electronique professionelle	65%
	Nucleaire	50%
	Construction navale	50%

Share By Sectors

Budget 1982 des marches d'etudes de la Direction des Recherches Techniques de l'Armement (DGA/DRET): 17 Milliards deF	Electronique	25%
	Nucleaire	20
	Engins	20
	Aeronautique	20
	Divers	15

Foreign Trade in Arms

Exports	Imports	New Export Orders	Share of World Arms Trade		
			USA	USSR	FRANCE
30 Billion F	1 Billion F	42 Billion F	38%	30%	10%

Source: Christian Stoffaes, "Industrial Policy in High Technology Industries: The French Experience," unpublished paper presented at Brookings Institution Conference on Industrial Policy in France and its implications for the United States, September 27–28, 1984.

4

Federal Republic
of Germany

Introduction

No government policies were discovered in the Federal Republic of Germany that had been designed explicitly to aid individual communities or firms in adjusting to reduced military spending. Indeed, successive West German governments have emphasized repeatedly that such adjustment is essentially a private, not a public, responsibility. Thus, in responding to questions posed in the Bundestag (Parliament) by its own party spokesmen concerning conversion of armaments production, the prior Social Democratic administration observed that ". . . the production and marketing of all kinds of goods are the responsibility of business in a free enterprise economy. Adaptation to continuous structural change in the economy is a task for enterprises with the maintenance or change in productive capacity remaining primarily a business decision. This is as true for arms producers as it is for others."[1]

This rather severe sounding policy is better understood against the background of Federal German government policy toward armaments production and export during the relatively brief life of the Federal Republic. As traced in the above-mentioned government statement, West Germany consciously avoided the reconstruction of publicly managed armaments companies and/or a specialized armaments industry. It was decided, rather, to encourage armaments production within private, technically similar, civil industry. To the extent to which this policy was successful, the geographic distribution of arms production would resemble that of the civil industries in which it was imbedded and would represent only a small part of the overall capacity of these industrial sectors. Thus, in 1982, employment in arms production of some 200,000 to 250,000 people represented just under 3% of total employment in manufacturing and less than 1% of the total work force. Arms orders then accounted for under 1% of sales in most industrial sectors, with a few obvious exceptions.

The government has also attempted to discourage the development of "excessive" concentration or expansion in the armaments industry through selectivity in the placement of orders by the armed forces and by a restrictive arms export policy involving non-NATO member countries. It has encouraged producers of armaments to utilize their facilities for civil products, as well, and generally, to diversify their output. Thus, the aircraft/aerospace and shipbuilding industries have both received financial aid from the government to strengthen their civil branches. Such industry-specific aid remains the exception rather than the rule and high government officials still prefer policy measures which improve the overall industrial environment for private decision making rather than providing aid for specific industries in order to "rescue managements from the consequences of their own poor judgment."

The German government forsees no sharp reductions in the need for armaments capacity in the near future. Thus, conversion of arms production to civil uses "can only be a result of agreement on disarmament but not a means to achieve it." The government's response to the questions from the Parliamentary Social Democrats concluded that there was "no possibility to prepare now for conversion that would result from (future possible) agreements on disarmament" and rejected "the establishment of a 'government commission' to plan such conversion as inefficient and unlikely to yield new insights or possibilities."

On the other hand, while unilateral German disarmament is not a likely development, cycles do occur in the procurement of major weapons systems and lower utilization of weapons production facilities can be expected in the near future. Thus, the production run of the Franco-German "Alphajet," a military trainer/ground attack aircraft, has been completed and the inventory of the multinational, multi-role combat aircraft designated "Tornado" will reach planned strength in the later 1980s. There has already been a decline in the acquisition of naval warships and production of the popular Leopard 2 tank is scheduled to end in the 1986–1987 period. According to Ministry of Defense officials, while new programs are coming in they are unlikely to fill the gap. A new major battle tank is not planned before the late 1990s and serious work on future combat aircraft will not begin before the early to mid-1990s. Thus, a change in the composition of military output in the next few years should challenge the adjustment capabilities of German industry and the laissez-faire policy of the German government.[2]

The government does recognize a responsibility to make serious defense plans in advance, to keep industry sufficiently informed to permit it to prepare for changes in military procurement, and to avoid abrupt shifts which might prove disruptive and cause social distress. Its formal position is one of confidence, based on past successes of German arms producers in managing considerable capacity adaptations to changes in both the level and structure of the defense budget. It also takes the position that existing conventional measures to aid structural change and unemployment are adequate to facilitate the conversion of armaments capacity to civil production.

Before examining such policies it might be appropriate to comment on current views in West Germany concerning the degree of success attained in reaching the ambitious goals outlined above concerning armaments production. In late 1984 and early 1985 concern was being expressed about an overconcentration of weapons production capacity, both geographically and industrially.

Thus, the modern heavy weapons industry is highly concentrated in Bavaria, particularly in and around Munich. This area contains many of the production facilities of the aerospace giant, Messerschmitt-Bölkow-Blohm (MBB), its smaller competitor, Dornier; tank producer, Krauss-Maffei; the electronics giant, Siemens; and the aircraft engine producer, Motoren-und-Turbinen-Union (MTU). These are only the most prominent names on a long list of military equipment producers in the Munich area.

Another related matter was receiving much press attention at year end, 1985: Should MBB be allowed to buy a controlling interest in Kraus-Maffei shareholdings? The Ministry of Defense is apparently concerned that such a sale might overconcentrate defense production in the hands of MBB, even if MBB participation is to be indirect via a special holding company formed by several banks. The West German Monopolies Commission also had expressed concern.[3]

These observations are not raised in a critical vein but only to portray accurately current attitudes in the Federal Republic of Germany on these relevant issues. Thus, the goal of limiting concentration is not an easy objective and the 59% of MBB's turnover represented by armaments in 1984[4] is appreciably lower than the military portion of sales of certain of its European and American competitors.

Background on German Industrial Policy[5]

At the end of World War II, Germany was a defeated and divided country with much of its industrial plant in ruins. After the formation of the Federal Republic, an early and important goal was the rebuilding of its economy, necessarily without its traditional ties to industry in the eastern part of the country. Since its strength had traditionally been based on heavy industry it was natural for German policy in the 1950s to spur investment in the historically important steel industry, and its complements, iron ore and coal. The electric power industry also received aid. This assistance was granted essentially through favorable tax provisions.

The story of the German "Economic Miracle" is familiar today and the West German economy indeed performed in an impressive manner through the 1950s and into the mid-1960s with minimal government direction. It was not the only success story, however, and by the mid-1960s, French and Japanese "indicative" (non-coercive) planning also was being widely proclaimed as the key to impressive economic growth in those countries. The European Economic Commission became a strong advocate of economic planning and the topic was projected to the top rung of discussion by the publication of a major document by the EEC; the "Memorandum on the Community's Program of Action for the Second Stage."[6]

Despite the good record of performance by the German economy and the market orientation of its policymakers, the Federal Republic moved early to follow France and Japan in adopting microeconomic strategies designed to forward its macroeconomic objectives. The Stability and Growth Act of 1966 provided a means of obtaining a consensus among what the Germans call the "social partners," labor, business, and the government on economic goals and the means to attain them. The process was called "concertation" and brought together for private conferences top government officials and highly placed labor and business representatives.

The economic interest groups in the West German economy are highly organized. Thus, the head organization of German industry, the Federation of German Industries (Bundesverband der Deutschen Industrie—BDI) is an umbrella organization of 37 parent industrial trade associations at the national level, in turn comprising over 500 trade and regional associations. There is also the Confederation of German Employers' Associations (Bundesvereinigung der Deutschen Arbeitgeberverbande—BDA) which represents the social and wage policy interests of all German business and which negotiates with the powerful and similarly organized trade unions. Also relevant are the Chambers of Industry and Commerce, regional business organizations which represent the overall interests of trade and industry in their respective districts. Of particular interest to an American observer is the fact that all enterprises are required by law to become members of the Chamber in their particular region. The top organization of these Chambers is the Association of German Chambers of Industry and Commerce (Deutscher Industrieund Handelstag—DHI).[7] These organizations play a much more important role in policy formulation than the typical American trade association and provide a powerful vehicle for the expression of their members' viewpoints.

Such a highly organized structure of interest groups raised concerns that concertation would produce a protectionist anti-market direction. As Franko points out, this did not occur but rather a consensus was reached that to preserve and expand the economic gains attained by the mid-1960s, "higher labor costs had to be reflected in higher skilled, more knowledge intensive production (and) . . . low skill, low value added products in which low wage countries were developing a comparative advantage would have to be phased out."[8]

As German industrial policy has evolved, the main actors have become the Ministry of Economics, which has demonstrated an aversion to providing large subsidies to traditional industries in structural decline (steel, coal, textiles, shipbuilding) and has forced rationalization (mergers and capacity reductions) upon them; and the Ministry of Research and Technology (Bundesministerium für Forschung und Technologie—BMFT) formed in 1972 to administer support for high technology industry.

Technology and Science[9]

The formation of BMFT represented a new departure for German policy concerning high technology and science. Prior to 1972 there had been a major drive to close the gap between Germany and other industrial states in such areas as nuclear energy, aerospace, and computer technology. Such large scientific programs were administered by the Ministry of Scientific Research and the Ministry of Atomic Questions (Bundesministerium für Atomfragen). Basic research was conducted in the universities and financed by the respective German state (Länder) while the federal government supported more applied research in various institutes. By the late 1960s, following a German government decision to use its R&D support to aid the competitiveness of its industry, noncommercial activities became the responsibility of the Ministry of Education and Science (created in 1960), while the BMFT undertook the support of high-technology industry.

By 1982, the Federal and Länder governments together budgeted about $8 billion for research and development. While most of this R&D support is provided across the board on a non-industry-specific basis, the aerospace and electronics industries represent significant exceptions. These will be discussed below. In recent years, what is described as the "general promotion of knowledge"; received the largest share of government R&D expenditure (almost 41%) with energy ranking second with 16%. Improving industrial productivity and technology rated third at 12%. Both direct and indirect support are provided for commercial R&D activities: the former consists of the actual financing of R&D projects while the latter involves an array of mechanisms whose goal is to increase actual research, development, and innovation conducted within German firms. Such indirect measures are growing and are conducted via tax benefits for R&D, financial assistance from the Risk Financing Associations (WFG), and Technologically Oriented Firms program (TOU), the microelectronics program, aid to small and medium-sized firms, and the technology transfer program—all described below.[10]

As noted above, the BMFT is the principal organ for conducting technology policy in the FRG and in 1982 was the conduit for 90% of direct government support for commercial R&D. Recipients of its grants were primarily industrial and commercial firms (78%), with the balance going to independent laboratories (11%), universities (8%), and others (3%).[11] BMFT support varies with the distance of a project from the commercial market. Thus, while as a general rule 50% is the maximum funding for a project, an exception is made for very large projects and those close to the basic research end of the spectrum, with 100% support possible. If commercially successful, repayment may be requested. With government support for private R&D, the question of intellectual property rights arises. Under the West German system, the government may use, free of charge, the results of R&D it has financed and has licenses to patents growing out of such research. The BMFT itself does not hold patents but organizations performing government financed R&D must license any patents resulting from it to others wishing to utilize them for a reasonable fee.[12] If over 50% of a project's costs are funded by the BMFT, all results must be published and are therefore in the public domain. Disclosure requirements are more modest for projects receiving less than 50% support. Organizations reluctant to make full disclosure are consequently motivated to keep the level of government support below the 50% level.[13] The largest share of BMFT funds in 1984 was budgeted for energy (39.1%). Space activities received 11.4%, while aviation and electronics industry grants were 2.5% and 4.1%, respectively.

Aid for Particular Technologies. The FRG has initiated several programs to assist what are considered priority technologies. Most are close to commercialization with almost 75% of such financing going to microelectronics, 15% to raw material refining technology, 5% to health care, and about 5% for waste disposal. Grants under the microelectronics program provide up to D.M. 800,000 for new product or process development.[14]

Aid for Smaller Enterprises. Research activities by small and medium-sized enterprises are administered by the Ministry of Economics. These include a special program designed to support R&D in West Berlin, a subsidy to cover R&D personnel expenses, and a mechanism to induce external research contracting by such firms. The orientation of these programs reflects a desire to balance off the fact that BMFT aid most often goes to large firms.[15] To qualify for this general program firms must employ under 2,000 people, have an annual sales turnover of less than D.M. 1 million, and not be a subsidiary of a large firm. It should be noted that medium-sized firms occasionally occupy a very important place in the West German economy. The Zeiss optical company provides an example. Grants under these programs totaled just under D.M. 410 million, or $169 million, in 1982.[16]

Information Transmission. The federal government has accepted the responsibilty of attempting to transmit potentially relevant technological information to industry. Funding comes largely from the information and documentation program of the BMFT. The Rationalization Commission (RKW) also transfers information and advises firms, doing some limited research on its own. The RKW is funded by federal and Länder governments, industry contributions, and contract income.[17] In 1984, according to the Ministry of Finance, the federal share of support for this program was expected to be just over D.M. 12 million.

Tax, Credit, and Direct Financial Assistance

Thus far the roles of the Ministry of Economics and the BMFT in conducting West German industrial and science policy have been emphasized. It is appropriate now to introduce the remaining institutional participant, the government-owned Kreditanstalt für Wiederaufbau (KFW) which provides export credits for trade with developing countries. Direct funding assistance is also provided via public procurement policies by both the federal government and the Länder which favor German products, and credit arrangements and guarantees which support small, new ventures. All of these will be discussed in turn.

By the mid-1970s the Federal Republic was strongly supporting industries toward the high-technology end of the industrial spectrum and, despite the drive toward rationalization in the more traditional industries, was also providing aid to depressed sectors. While political realities contributed to this rather ambivalent stance, the German government's support for civilian research and development reached 1.1% of gross domestic product in 1974, the highest level among the six major states of Western Europe. At the same time, its aid to depressed industries such as coal mining, textiles, and clothing, though substantial, was the lowest in the EEC.[18]

The general format of government support to West German industry at that time is shown in Table 4.1. Regional policy has been a more important device for providing government aid than specific industrial subsidies and such regional assistance has been rather widely dispersed among industries. The one outstanding exception to this pattern appears in an industry of great importance for defense, the aircraft sector, which received government subsidies equal to approximately 23.5% of value added.[19] Alternatively, aircraft received no effective tariff protection, although it is a sector which typically benefits from public procurement preferences.[20] The principal beneficiaries of tariff protection have been the pulp and paper, nonferrous metals, textiles, clothing, and paper products industries. This pattern of aid continued through the end of the decade with the bulk of government assistance going to support regional programs, and coal mining, aircraft, and shipbuilding.

The profile of West German government aid to industry appears to diverge along a line set by level of technology. Thus, essentially weak sectors characterized by high labor and raw materials-intensive production receive tariff and quota protection from foreign competition while high-technology sectors have been the beneficiaries of public procurement preferences and to some extent, research and development support (especially in aerospace and electronics). Of course, public procurement preferences represent a more important form of support where public sector purchases are significant, and this condition prevails in the FRG with government outright ownership or participation in the communication system, most electrical utilities, and the national airline. For various reasons, however, public procurement preferences appear to have become less important in the 1980s.[21]

Regional considerations play a very important role in West German industrial policy, and it is impossible to discuss government subsidies via tax policy,[22] direct financial aid, or even rationalization without noting this. Thus, with the exception of coal, shipbuilding, and steel, industrial tax advantages are usually aimed at particular regions. Even here, these three industries are not ubiquitous and demonstrate regional concentration. Total tax benefits to German industry in 1982 from both federal and Länder governments totaled D.M. 10.9 billion or $3.8 billion, 79% of which were regional subsidies.[23] Most of the tax benefits which fall outside the category of regional aid are not industry-specific in that eligibility is based upon company size as in assistance to small firms, and/or the encouragement of research and development. Tax credits of up to 20% of research and development expenditures up to D.M. 500,000 and 7.5% of such expenditures above that figure are available. The D.M. 500,000 breakpoint is clearly designed to help smaller enterprises. This is also reflected in the provisions which permit firms to receive any unused tax credit (because their tax liabilities are less than the allowable credit) as a direct payment. Such federal and Länder support was in the range of $115–130 million in the early 1980s.[24]

Industry-specific tax assistance is found in coal mining, steel, and ship-building. These industries appear repeatedly in all lists of West German government aid going to specific industries rather than allocated to regions or to industry-wide functions such as encouragement of research and development and energy conservation. Thus, of the $1.5 billion of direct financial aid to industry in 1982, coal mining received over 35%, steel 10%, and shipbuilding 6.5%. Unlike the gestures to help depressed traditional industries, the aircraft industry's share of 11% may be viewed as aid to a strategic high-technology sector.[25] Table 4.2 provides more recent data on federal government subsidies and tax breaks.

The government's financial aid is provided as grants, loan guarantees, and low-interest loans. The latter are of interest since they are farmed out to the banking system. Thus, loans are directed through the Central Bank (Bundesbank) to one of the major commercial banks (Dresdner Bank, Deutsche Bank, or Commerz Bank) which in turn select specific firms to receive the loans.[26]

Participation by the West German government in the ownership of industry has not received much attention, particularly in view of its widely publicized commitment to a free enterprise philosophy. However, the government's participation is substantial in a number of important firms and industries. The federal government has been a majority shareholder of Lufthansa and a visible partner in the ownership of the shipbuilding and auto industries. Government participation is not limited to the federal level. The Länder governments of Bavaria and Hamburg are important shareholders of Messerschmitt-Bölkow-Blohmn, and Bremen owned 26.4% of VFW-Fokker before the two companies ended their merger and VFW (Vereinigte Flugtechnische Werke) became a wholly owned subsidiary of MBB at the beginning of 1983.[27] According to Donges,[28] five policy objectives provided the underlying rationale for West German government ownership of industry:

1. increasing employment in depressed regions;
2. avoiding private monopoly;
3. providing low-income housing;
4. speeding innovation; and
5. pursuing self sufficiency in strategic materials.

However, there has been some disappointment with the results of state ownership and there are current signs of a move to reduce it. Thus, there has been talk of reducing the combined federal/state ownership in Lufthansa from almost 80% to around 55%.[29] After some delay the federal government in the summer of 1986 announced plans to sell all its shares in Volkswagen, the auto multinational, and in VEBA, a large energy and chemical group.[30]

Export Promotion and Insurance. The West German program of export promotion and insurance appears to utilize a public-private partnership approach. Thus, a consortium of the firms Hermes and Treuarbeit administers loan guarantees and export credit insurance. Traditionally, only limited export insurance and financing has been provided for exports to other industrialized countries. Long-term financing for exports of German heavy equipment comes from a consortium of 52 essentially private sector banks known as the Ausfuhrkredit Aktiengesellschaft (AKA) which receives government support. Since 1973, however, the most rapidly growing markets for German products have been found in nonindustrialized countries, particularly the OPEC group. In trade with such countries public financing and guarantees are more important. These are provided by the government-owned Kreditanstalt für Wiederaufbau (KFW).[31] As recently as 1980, however, AKA and KFW government-aided loans accounted for under 1% of exports of the FRG.[32] Of interest is that the West German shipbuilding and aircraft industries receive better terms on their loans than export credit financing otherwise available. Loans to support export sales of ships and aircraft were a significant portion of KFW's export credits in the early 1980s.[33] Since 1975, export credits received by small and medium-sized firms have also been eligible for guarantee by the Länder.[34]

KFW, in addition to its role of guarantor of export credits also serves as the West German investment bank and in this capacity provides domestic loans, primarily to small and medium-sized firms and for environmental protection measures. KFW loans are widely distributed among industries.

Capital for Innovative Firms. In the belief that German capital markets tend to be overly conservative, the federal government has instituted several programs in support of innovative activities. The programs tend to assist small innovative firms in high technology areas, without respect to industry. The Economics Ministry is responsible for the Capital Participation Societies and the First Innovation Program, while the Ministry of Research and Technology (BMFT) administers the Risk Financing Association and the Technologically Oriented Firm program (TOU).

Capital Participation Societies, known as KBGs for the German initials, receive three-fourths of their funding as loans from the KFW and obtain the remainder from private sources. They can make loans directly, or assume an equity position in small firms. There has been some criticism of KBGs for excessive caution in supporting higher risk projects.[35] The KFW made available the equivalent of $8.4 million to KBGs in 1982 for the encouragement of small and medium-sized businesses at very liberal terms.[36]

Commercial development of new technologies was aided under the First Innovation Program which provided interest-free loans for half the cost of such development with the loan becoming a grant if no profits were earned on the project for 10 years. Eligible projects had to involve truly new innovations in the Federal Republic with some reasonable chance of market acceptance, serve a social need, and be viewed as too uncertain by conventional sources of private financing. In January 1984, the government halted this program due to budgetary stringency.

In 1975, a consortium of German banks organized the Risk Financing Association (WFG) to buy into small innovative companies and provide managerial and technical assistance. The government guaranteed three-fourths of the funds invested by the banks in the WFG. The plan called for sale by the banks at a profit of equity shares of successful firms. However, only a small number of firms have been involved in the program. The conservatism of the banks in the consortium and the underdeveloped market for equities of small and medium-sized firms in the Federal Republic are viewed as major contributors to the failure of the program.[37]

The Technologically Oriented Firms program (TOU) is designed to aid firms beginning to operate in high technology areas with consulting assistance, grants for up to three-fourths of development costs, and loan guarantees covering up to 80% of initial capital and marketing costs. It demonstrates a curious geographical dichotomy, being a national program for microelectronics but servicing other industrial sectors only in the six regions where the BMFT (Bundesministerium für Forschung und Technologie), the sponsoring organization, already operates consulting activities. Funding for the First Innovation, WFG, and TOU programs has been very small and the 1983 projected level of support was not expected to reach $8 million.[38]

Regional Policy[39]

Regional economic policy reflects the divided nature of the German nation and the prolonged isolation of West Berlin. Thus, West Berlin and the Zonal Border Area (Zonenrandgebiet)—a 40 kilometer-wide belt of territory running along the borders with East Germany and Czechoslovakia qualify for a higher investment allowance under the German Regional Incentive program than other eligible areas. The rationale rests on the argument that these areas are negatively influenced by the lack of an economic "hinterland." Special efforts for these areas also are justified by the West German constitutional provision that all regions of the country should enjoy the same standard of living.

Since 1969, the federal government and the states (Länder) have shared responsibility for regional policy. In that year a constitutional mechanism was established to coordinate their respective actions. It is known as the Joint Task for the Improvement of Regional Economic Structures (Gemeinschaftsaufgabe "Verbesserung Der Regionalen Wirtschaftsstruktur"). An annual framework plan (Rahmenplan) to coordinate regional policy is drawn up by a joint planning committee.

The basic component of the German regional incentive program is the investment allowance (Investitionszulage), a project-related capital grant which can also be taken as an allowance against tax if the recipient prefers. The beneficial award rule of 10% of eligible expenditure applies in the Zonal Border Area as noted above, and 8.75% elsewhere in the "GA areas";

those designated eligible under the Gemeinschaftsaufgabe. Something over 28% of the national population (including that of West Berlin) and about half of the surface area of the country (also including West Berlin) are now included in the GA areas. The Zonal Border Area itself contains 11.5% of the national population. Contained within the GA areas are 259 growth points (Schwerpunktorte) which receive the bulk of regional aid programs.

In addition to investment allowance, an investment grant (Investitionszuschuss) is also available from the funds of the GA program. The grant combined with other specific regional forms of aid such as the investment allowance, must fall inside a matrix of maximum preferential rates. Thus, the matrix contains rate limits ranging between 10 and 25% of eligible fixed investment, depending upon location and type of project. Preferential rates apply to the Zonal Border Area, particular types of growth points, and setting-up projects and extensions. Furthermore, there are several incentives which exist only within the Zonal Border Area: a freight-transport subsidy and a special depreciation allowance of up to 50% of the cost of machinery and up to 40% of buildings, over and above basic straight line depreciation.

Finally, there are the "European Recovery Program regional soft loans" (ERP-Regionaldarlehen), essentially automatic, project-related loans available only to small- or medium-sized firms for projects *not* eligible for the investment allowance or investment grant. These basically finance local services (like trade, crafts, restaurants etc.). Again the Zonal Border areas are favored.

In most Länder, yet other grants are available which coordinate with the GA program. After a recent review, the coverage of the GA areas has been substantially reduced. However, the 1982 Framework Plan contained a Steel Location Program which added three new steel closure areas on a temporary basis: Bochum, Dortmund, and Duisburg. The Bremen area has also been declared eligible for the investment allowance through 1987. This was a response to worsening unemployment reflecting declines in the shipbuilding and steel industries.

It appears that regional policy in the Federal Republic is increasingly being used to alleviate problems resulting from sectoral declines which happen to be spatially-concentrated. West German regional policy outside the Zonal Border Area is relatively modest when compared to other countries in the European Economic Community.

The extensive array of policies described above seem to have evolved to meet particular problems as they arose rather than to form the components of a coherent industrial policy. Indeed, recent government responses to questions raised in the Parliament (Bundestag) by Social Democratic spokesmen concerning regional economic development and the creation of new jobs through "an active industrial policy" stress that the necessary innovation, risk taking, and investment require a reduction in state intervention and reliance on a market-oriented policy.[40]

Expectations of FRG Defense Spending in the Near Term

The general expectation in the West German aerospace industry was for military spending to remain stable or possibly increase by a small amount to meet NATO commitments and to compensate for inflation. The only two military aircraft programs on the horizon are a successor to the Franco-German Transall military transport aircraft; and the European Fighter Aircraft program.[41]

The relatively small number of potential major projects in the near term suggests a worsening of the ever-present procurement cycle of individual programs. Thus, in 1984 the RB-199 engine program for the Tornado aircraft accounted for about three-fifths of the total sales of Motoren-und Turbinen-Union of Munich. After 1988, this share is expected to fall to less than 20% when the series production of this engine is phased out. However, since the next military fighter program of like magnitude will not begin until after 1992, the resulting gap will somehow have to be bridged. Unless cycles in military procurement apply across the board, which is rare, changes in the product composition of military equipment purchases will have differing impacts on particular firms. Thus, increases in the purchases of helicopters, missiles, and naval vessels will be of little value to firms whose principal product consists of fighter aircraft.

Degree of Dependence on the Military Customer

The figures on employment and sales dependency on military contracts at the beginning of this chapter on West Germany were taken from the 1982 government statement entitled Konversion Von Rustungskapazitaten. More recent data were secured from meetings and correspondence with government and industry officials, and from the German press.[42] Thus, the West German Ministry of Defense and the West German Industry Association estimate the number of employees working in the armaments sector at between 200,000 and 300,000. While precise statistics are not available a figure of 250,000 is most often encountered. The volume of contracts placed with industry by the Defense Ministry in 1985 is estimated at about D.M. 20 billion for slightly more than 1% of GNP. Arms contracts constitute almost exactly 2% of manufacturing industry sales. In the past few years the bulk of military investment has gone for major weapons systems and second generation military equipment, such as the Tornado multi-role combat aircraft, the Leopard 2, Roland and Gepard tanks, a new generation of fighters, frigates, patrol boats, field howitzers, guided missiles, and the AWACS early warning system.

Major German military producers' sales to the Armed Forces fell into a range which spreads from a third to 85% of total sales with the Diehl group at the low end and Krauss-Maffei AG of Munich at the high mark. The military share of 1984 sales of West Germany's largest arms producer,

Messerchmitt-Bölkow-Blohm GmbH of Munich was placed at 60% by the Suddeutsche Zeitung[43] and at roughly 50% by an MBB executive.

Apparently the civil portion has been increasing slightly over the years. Dornier's military share at 50% has declined from 65 to 70% in 1977–1978. Mototen-und Turbinen-Union München GmbH (MTU) has always been highly dependent on military programs. The 1984 contribution of such programs at 78% of total sales was down somewhat from 80% in 1983, 86% in 1980, and 93% in 1974.

Some confusion surrounds the military share of sales of Rheinmetall AG of West Berlin/Dusseldorf, an important tank and gun producer. Although an official of the West German Ministry of Defense noted that Rheinmetall was "almost 100% dependent on the military," the above-cited newspaper account attributed only 37% of its sales to the military. The same two sources also appear to differ on the military dependence of major electronics firms with the MOD official stressing a very low level industry-wide figure of about 5% while the press account describes AEG Telefunken and Siemens as having "both earned major parts of their turnover from military contracts." To some extent these differences may be due to differences in billing routines. Thus, a German aerospace executive noted that turnover figures from large defense and space contracts are often billed after two or more years of performance in one large amount while civil programs are billed on a continuous basis. Therefore, percentages based on a particular year can be distorted and rapidly changing while true tendencies can only be seen over a number of years.

Plans to Increase Civil Market Share. Correspondence on this issue was conducted with the three major West German aerospace firms, MBB, Dornier, and MTU. Each of the three had experienced an increase in the share of total sales attributed to civil markets but the engine maker, MTU, had the largest military dependence at 78% of total sales in 1984. However, the company is planning to increase its civil share to over 33% by 1988. This goal will be attained by efforts on the part of MTU to increase its activities in the civil engine market. It is currently participating in such civil projects as the CF 6-50, CF 6-80, JT8D-200, PW 2037 and V 2500. Parts are being produced for all of these engines except the V 2500 which is still in the development phase. The CF 6 is a large two-spool turbofan engine which can power such wide body aircraft as the Airbus A-300 and A-310, Boeing 747 and 767, and McDonnell-Douglas DC10. MTU shares 7 to 12%, depending on specific engine type, and cooperates with General Electric, SNECMA, Rolls-Royce, Volvo-Flygmotor and Fiat Aviazione. The JT8D-200 is a two-spool turbofan engine of medium size which will power the McDonnell-Douglas MD-80 aircraft. Cooperation will be with Pratt & Whitney of United Technologies and Volvo Flygmotor. MTU's share will be 12.5% of this engine. The PW 2037 is a two-spool turbofan engine to power the Boeing 757. MTU's share will be 11.2% in cooperation with Pratt & Whitney and Fiat Aviazione. The V2500 will be a two-spool turbofan engine of moderate thrust designed to power the Airbus A-320, Boeing 737-500 and

7-7, and the McDonnell-Douglas MD-80RE. MTU's share will be 12.1% in cooperation with Pratt & Whitney, Rolls-Royce, Fiat Aviazione, and JACE, a consortium of Japanese engine makers.

In addition to the production of civil aeroengines, MTU München also is active in the overhaul and repair of engines via its wholly-owned subsidiary, MTU Maintenance GmbH. These operations have grown appreciably in the last few years. Other wholly owned subsidiaries of MTU Munchen are Chemie-und Textil-Gesellschaft mbH Friedrichshafen, a real estate administration company and MTU Versicherungsvermittlungs-und Wirtschaftsdienst-Gesellschaft mbH which handles all insurance affairs of the MTU group.

MTU München Affiliates include:

- Aktiengesellschaft Kuhnle, Kopp and Kausch (KKK) which develops, manufactures and markets fans, compressors, steam turbines, and exhaust turbo-chargers;
- MTU Turbomeca S.A.R.L. which coordinates the development, production, sales, and product support activities for engines produced under cooperation agreements;
- Turbo-Union Ltd. which coordinates the production of the RB-199 jet engine for the Tornado combat aircraft;
- IAE International AeroEngines AG, founded in 1983 by five aeroengine manufacturers from Europe, the US, and Japan to coordinate the development, production, and sales of the V 2500 engine for a new generation of 150-seater aircraft; and MTU Informationssysteme GmbH, the latest acquisition which engages in real estate and plant leasing and also operates in the data processing area where it offers consultation, software, and computer services.

MTU Friedrichshafen, the other half of the MTU group, operates subsidiaries in North America, Brazil, Argentina, Singapore, and Australia, all of which are engaged in marketing, assembly, maintenance, and repair of MTU Friedrichsafen products. Despite the growing number of administrative subdivisions, it does not appear that MTU has strayed far afield from its principal operations as producer of aeroengines.

The last few years have seen substantial reorganization of corporate management and organizational structure at MBB. The goals were to integrate the operating units more closely into the basic corporate policymaking processes and to more rapidly and smoothly turn promising ideas into saleable products. Two new corporate sectors were created: Industrial Products, and Industrial Energy and Process Technology. The first has responsibility for activities in the fields of data systems technology, industrial electonics, automation technology, transportation technology, medical technology, and high performance composite materials. The second will coordinate MBB activities in bioengineering, thermal energy systems, wind power, vacuum superinsulation, photovoltaics, and environmental protection. Both sectors will be responsible to link MBB diversification activities closely to the requirements of the market and to explore product lines apart from the company's classical aerospace emphasis.

Three developments are of special interest: development and production work in what are called wheel-on rail technologies—high-speed subways and railway trains; the pilot testing of a wind power plant developed for the Federal Ministry of Research and Technology; and initiating the operation of a pilot plant for the series production of auto parts made of fibre composite materials. These activities have been transferred from the Helicopter and Transport Division where they originated to the new Industrial Energy and Process Technology, and Industrial Products sectors.

MBB has also been very active in the full array of European space activities and involved in such civil activities as the airbus, the F-28 Fellowship with Fokker of the Netherlands and the successor F-100 and F-50 versions, and the Franco-Italian ATR-42 commercial aircraft.

The patience, careful thought, and willingness to bear risk necessary for successful diversification were stressed by a Dornier executive. Thus:

> This increase of share of civilian market sales—as you can well imagine—did not just happen by chance. It was part of our company policy during the last 10 years. The long-term planning of our DOD gave enough early warning that missing defence business had to be compensated by other and, therefore, civilian programs. This policy meant taking in subcontracting work in Airbus on not too advantageous and risk-sharing terms conditioned to many millions of Marks of investment in infrastructure, special machinery and tooling out of our own pocket (these kinds of costs normally are carried by the government, if military programs). It meant also to invest heavily not only for R&D, series preparation and all the work in process to run a program like our Dornier 228 Commuter Aircraft with a return on investment (break-even-point) in a very distant and uncertain future and it also meant to push ahead with the (kidney stone) Lithotripter entering a so-called "new game" like the medical market (diversification). To expand our traditional textile machinery field is a comparatively easy "game". Therefore, yes, the company has plans to increase the civilian market share and will have to continue in the future to do so.

The pressure for diversification in the West German aerospace industry reflects, in part, the high cost of new military aircraft with a resulting drop in the number of units ordered by the military. For example, the West German Air Force had 624 F-104 Starfighters, now operates 322 Tornado aircraft, and is unlikely to buy more than about 170 successors to the F-4 Phantom (tentatively designated Jager 90, the German name for the European Fighter Aircraft).[44] This trend has meant fewer workshop hours for military production.

Arms Exports and Collaborative Ventures

An obvious way to adjust to a reduction of the domestic market is to seek markets elsewhere via exports. For political reasons the Federal Republic of Germany has imposed rather stringent requirements on military exports destined to be shipped outside of the NATO countries and other allied or neutral countries such as Australia, New Zealand, Japan, Switzerland, Austria, and Sweden. When the destination is elsewhere, the government considers each request on a case-by-case basis and will permit such shipments only where a vital national interest of West Germany is seen as involved. In the past, it has been easier to export ships than tanks or combat aircraft. Saudi Arabia attempted to buy Leopard 2 tanks a few years ago and after lengthy discussions the request was rejected. There have been occasional suspicions raised over the years concerning the administration of FRG arms export regulations. Thus, it has been rumored that German submarines have been sold to buyers in the UK and then transshipped to Latin America. Strict enforcement of the present rules would appear to rule out military exports as a realistic alternative to sales to the West German armed forces. However, a tripling of German arms exports since 1982 has given rise to a renewed debate on the effectiveness of export restrictions. While some of the increase represented delivery of naval vessels to Argentina and Colombia which had been approved under the previous Social Democratic government, recent decisions to allow the Association of South East Asian Nations (ASEAN) easier access to German weapons and the sale of seventy-two Tornados to Saudi Arabia and of eight to Oman have sparked renewed debate.[45]

At the end of World War II severe restrictions were placed upon German production of armaments. For a decade following the end of the War, for example, Germany was prohibited from most aerospace activities. When the restrictions were lifted the Federal Republic had fallen behind its neighbors in aerospace and jet engine technology. Hence, it was eager to participate in collective ventures with the hope that such involvement would help restore German talents in the aircraft industry. The story of the importance to Germany of its participation in the European consortium producing the F-104 Starfighter under license has been told frequently. Later work on the F-4 and Tornado also was important in the restoration of West German talents in the aircraft industry.

To some extent participation in collaborative ventures yields advantages similar to outright exports. For example, important scale economies may be attained if the total production for the entire consortium is substantially larger than any of the individual national orders would have been. Also, if the product is sufficiently attractive to third parties, it may also attract export orders. However, in the opinion of some British observers, West German political inhibitions to arms exports have inhibited sales of the Tornado outside of the consortium of the FRG, UK, and Italy. (See note 45 for a more recent, contrary view.)

Industrial Perceptions of Government Aid Policies

While few, if any, of the programs described above were explicitly designed to aid the transfer of resources from military to civil production, some of them clearly could be useful in such a transition. Thus, the awareness of such programs by defense industry executives and their evaluation of the effectiveness of such programs would be of particular interest to this study. Questions to elicit such information were posed to executives of the three major West German aerospace firms. All responded with differing perspectives and degrees of detail.

The response from an MBB executive was the most brief and circumspect. It referred to a general government policy of encouraging firms to avoid complete or great dependence on military procurement, but noted that "depending on the specific area of activities, there must be exceptions to this policy." The respondent went on to note that he was "not aware of a specific programme beyond this general policy to introduce civil business into companies with high military content."

The MTU response stressed government concerns about the aerospace industry and various forms of financial aid available. Thus.

Politicians and governmental agencies are aware of the structural problems of the German aeronautical industry arising from the procurement cycles. There is close interaction between federal efforts and efforts of the individual states to cope with those problems.

The German cabinet has appointed one of its members, Staatssekretär Martin Gruner, to act as governmental coordinator for the structural problems of the German aeronautical industry. . . .The Ministry of Economy has supported for years a variety of commercial programs with interest-fee loans repayable in the event of program success. . . .MTU München got such repayable loans for 50% of its development share of the PW2037 engine (limited, however, to a maximum of 150 Mio. D.M.). The federal funding of the German portion of the Airbus program is even higher and covers up to 90% of the development costs.

The German Ministry of Technology also takes regard of the aeronautical industry's high technology aspects and supports certain research and technology projects. The funds are, however, limited (e.g., 355 Mio. D.M. between 1973 and 1982 for the total industry) and do generally not exceed 50% of the costs of each project.

The main effort, however, to settle structural aspects and problems as described above has to be borne by the industry itself. Therefore, the large companies like MBB, Dornier, and MTU have conducted long-term plans and have executed measures in time to avoid structural gaps or to limit the effects of business depression arising from up-and-downs in military programs. There are different possibilities to achieve a well-balanced program policy, for instance:

• the adequate selection of the program shares in collaborative programs;
• extension of civil activities;
• the diversification into other products; and
• endeavour to obtain subcontract for a limited time period.

Another industrialist emphasized his government's occasional stretching of its laissez-faire attitude and relaxation of its arms export regulations to assist firms and regions in particular distress, as well as the potential transferability of military technology to civil markets.

This question is a very difficult one to answer. Yes, there is aid, or better said, preference, to allocate military contracts to economically depressed regions like the shipbuilding industry in particular. Even our strict arms export regulations are handled by the government in a more flexible manner to allow, for instance, for export of submarines and frigates. But following the rules of what is called "Freie Marktwirtschaft" there is, at least to my knowledge, no established government policy to aid firms to adjust to reduced military spending because it's considered a free entrepreneurial decision to engage or disengage a company in military programs. On the other side . . . there is a free flow, a real two-way street so to say of technology and know-how between military and civil market-oriented programs in particular in R&D activities. It is no question that military technology programs paid for by the DOD can find civil-oriented applications and this is even part of this policy. As so often, even if many people do not want to hear that, the "war is the father of many (sometimes good) things."

Economic conditions in the world shipbuilding industry have been poor for the past few years and the West German industry has not been spared depression-like conditions, especially in the larger yards producing merchant ships, tankers, and off-shore drilling platforms. Thus, while reduced military spending has not been the cause of the problem, an important industry which is involved in defense production has found itself in serious economic distress. For example, in the fall of 1983 the West German shipbuilder, Howaldtswerke-Deutschewerft Aktiengesellschaft Hamburg und Kiel, found itself facing the discharge of 4000 employees, something which doesn't happen often or easily in Europe. The company's annual report made it clear that federal and Länder aid programs for the shipbuilding industry were known and utilized. Indeed, the maritime states of the Federal Republic adopted a promotion for the West German shipbuilding industry in September 1983.[46] This situation is one where the concentration of a particular distressed industry in a specific region (North Germany) allowed an overlapping of industry and region-specific aid. Curiously, some German shipyards have attempted to survive during a period of low demand for merchant vessels by increasing their military work.[47]

An official of the Federation of German Industries (Bundesverband der Deutschen Industrie) noted that several departments in the Federal Ministry of Defense correspond to some industry divisions. Such military departments are in a position to see where technology will develop in the next 10 to 15 years. Such information can be useful to industry as a basis for accurate planning. Indeed the Ministry of Defense may go further and fund R&D in industry as it has in the case of the Future Fighter Aircraft (now European Fighter Aircraft) project. This official added that there was no desire in the FRG to follow the French model of industrial policy with "constant running back and forth between the government side and the industry side."

With respect to the policies discussed above, this trade association official doubted that the regional aid organizations were particularly relevant to the issue of economic conversion, with the possible exception of the shipyards. He also spoke of some conflict between different government ministries; thus, he saw the Ministry of Research as trying to develop technologies and therefore being reluctant to approve projects for industry producers. On the other hand, the Ministry of Defense was seen as working with the Ministry of Research to get best results for defense needs. The BDI official saw the Defense Ministry as more interested now than the Ministry of Research since the latter fears it will lose some of its scarce funds to military projects if it is overly cooperative and doesn't "protect its turf."

He also emphasized that in his opinion true diversification was not so much a matter of military versus civil customers as it was public vs. private. In his view the goal should be to avoid too many public orders which cause a loss of flexibility if a firm's public contracts exceed some critical level of total sales. He felt that this risk was inherent in sales to all levels of government since government is dependent on administrative decisions which can lead to a quick reversal of longstanding policies leaving the supplier in a vulnerable position.

Summary

Although most explicitly stressing that adjustment to reduced military spending is a responsibility of industry the West German government recognizes the paramount strategic importance of several industries which it will not allow to fail. While it encourages such firms to plan ahead, to develop flexibility of response, and to collaborate with partners in friendly nations, the government is prepared to provide a safety net, if necessary, as a last resort. Such aid usually consists of the advance of funds by the government at low or zero interest rates which are expected to be repaid only if the use to which they are put is profitable (successful).

Faced with political inhibitions on the export of military equipment destined for countries outside a narrow range of NATO allies and other friendly and neutral states, the West German government has strongly encouraged collaborative weapons development and production. This has been particularly true in the aerospace industry where it applies as well to tactical missiles and civil aircraft. Enlarged production runs for multi-national products like the Tornado multi-role combat aircraft and the products of such consortia as Euromissile and Airbus Industrie have effectively enlarged the market for German industry and also established very useful contacts with firms in other countries.

Although resisting terms like "active industrial policy" it appears to an outside observer that the pieces from which such a policy could be constructed are already present. Thus, for certain strategic technologies and industries, aid is available from the federal and state governments. One can trace an idea far removed from commercial application receiving aid from the Federal

Ministry of Research and Technology and gradually moving from one ministry to another continuing to receive assistance as it moves closer to a marketable product. In some cases eventual public procurement may complete the story. Whether and how often such a scenario will be realized is, of course, another question.

Notes

1. The government response is entitled "Konversion von Rüstungskapazitäten" (Conversion of Armaments Capacity) and is dated 26 August 1982. It is a formal government response to questions raised by Parliamentary spokesmen of the Social Democratic Party on 31 March 1982.

2. A remarkably similar position was expressed more recently be a Christian Democratic Administration in a formal response to questions raised in the Bundestag about likely output levels in the West German defense industry in the near future and possible government measures to prevent unemployment if utilization of defense industry capacity falls. The exchange is found in *Drucksache* 10/2673, Deutscher Bundestag-10, Wahlperiode, December 21, 1984, p. 18.

3. *Suddeutsche Zeitung*, München, January 21, 1985—as translated in *The German Tribune: A Weekly Review of the German Press*, February 3, 1985, p. 8.

4. This figure was reported in *Rheinischer Merkur/Christ und Welt*, Bonn, December 21, 1984 as translated in *The German Tribune*, February 3, 1985, p. 8.

5. This section is based, in part, on Franko, *European Industrial Policy: Past, Present, and Future*, pp. 18–21 and 29–31, and Suomela, *et al.*, *US International Trade Commission, Foreign Industrial Targeting and Its Effect on US Industries, Phase II:*, pp. 68–93.

6. For a more complete discussion of this development, see Franko, *European Industrial Policy: Past, Present, and Future*, pp. 17–19.

7. The source of this information on West German organizations is an undated and untitled pamphlet published by The Federation of German Industries (BDI) in Cologne.

8. Franko, *European Industrial Policy: Past, Present, and Future*, p. 19.

9. This description of the evolution of German R&D and science policy is based on the Boston Consulting Group's *Framework For Swedish Industrial Policy* (Appendix 12, Germany), 1978, as quoted in Franko, *European Industrial Policy: Past, Present, and Future*, pp. 19–20.

10. Suomela, *et al.*, *US International Trade Commission, Foreign Industrial Targeting and Its Effect on US Industries, Phase II:*, pp. 82–84.

11. BMFT, "Wende in der Forschungspolitik," February, 1983, p. 25.

12. BMFT, "The Federal Ministry for Research and Technology," statement dated March 15, 1977, p. 4.

13. G. G. Heaton, "West Germany" in *National Support for Science and Technology*, Center for Policy Alternatives, Massachusetts Institute of Technology, 1976, pp. 73–74.

14. Suomela, *et al.*, *US International Trade Commission, Foreign Industrial Targeting and Its Effect on US Industries, Phase II:*, p. 87.

15. Heaton, "West Germany," pp. 73–74.

16. Suomela, *et al.*, *US International Trade Commission, Foreign Industrial Targeting and Its Effect on US Industries, Phase II:*, p. 87.

17. Heaton, "West Germany," pp. 78–79.

18. Franko, *European Industrial Policy: Past, Present, and Future*, pp. 4, 20.

19. The West German aerospace industry also benefits from government support for aerospace research and testing organizations. Thus, the Federal and State governments provided 80% of the 1982 budget of the German Aerospace Research and Experimental Establishment (DFVLR) and the federal government is the major shareholder of the IABG, nominally a commercial company which makes available its extensive testing equipment to industry, obviating the need for substantial private investment in duplicate and underutilized test facilities.

20. Even here it should be noted that the German national airline, Lufthansa, has been permitted to buy Boeing aircraft despite German participation in the European consortium, Airbus Industrie.

21. Suomela, *et al., US International Trade Commission, Foreign Industrial Targeting and Its Effect on US Industries, Phase II:*, p. 71.

22. The FRG publishes a unique document known as a "Subsidy Report" which estimates the subsidy equivalent of its tax benefits and financial aid to industry. The benefit value is computed as the loss of tax revenue resulting from such policies. Among the objectives of tax benefits are the preservation of firms and/or industries, helping them adjust to altered market conditions, encouraging their growth and efficiency, etc. (Suomela, *et al., US International Trade Commission, Foreign Industrial Targeting and Its Effect on US Industries, Phase II:*, p. 72.)

23. Suomela, *et al., US International Trade Commission, Foreign Industrial Targeting and Its Effect on US Industries, Phase II:*, p. 72. Public assistance to industry in the FRG must take into account the unique and significant role played by the German states or Länder.

24. Suomela, *et al., US International Trade Commission, Foreign Industrial Targeting and Its Effect on US Industries, Phase II:*, p. 72.

25. Suomela, *et al., US International Trade Commission, Foreign Industrial Targeting and Its Effect on US Industries, Phase II:*, p. 73.

26. Jack N. Behrman, "A Comparison of Approaches Toward Industrial Development," mimeographed, Appendix, pp. 17–19.

27. Behrman, "A Comparison of Approaches Toward Industrial Development," p. 19; *Business Europe*, October 7, 1983, pp. 313–314; K. D. Walter & R. D. Monsen, "State-Owned Business Abroad: New Competitive Threat," *Harvard Business Review*, Vol. 75 (No. 2), March-April 1979, p. 163.

28. J.B. Donges, "Industrial Policies in West Germany's 'Not-So-Market-Oriented' Economy," *World Economy*, Vol. 3 (No. 2), September 1980, p. 192.

29. The cut-back plan has recently become embroiled in political disagreement. See "West Germany Cuts Back Plan to Reduce its Stakes in Lufthansa, Other Concerns," *Wall Street Journal*, March 22, 1985, p. 24; and "West German Privatisation: Sell Now," *The Economist*, March 30, 1985, p. 77.

30. "Why West Germany is Selling Two Gems in the Crown Jewels," *The Economist*, July 5, 1986, pp. 52–55.

31. Franko, *European Industrial Policy: Past, Present, and Future*, pp. 29–31.

32. Organization for Economic Cooperation and Development, *The Export Credit Financing System*, (Paris: OECD, 1982), p. 114.

33. Suomela, *et al., US International Trade Commission, Foreign Industrial Targeting and Its Effect on US Industries, Phase II:*, p. 78.

34. Franko, *European Industrial Policy: Past, Present, and Future*, p. 31.

35. Heaton, "West Germany," pp. 73–74.

36. Suomela, *et al., US International Trade Commission, Foreign Industrial Targeting and Its Effect on US Industries, Phase II:*, p. 79–80.

37. Suomela, *et al., US International Trade Commission, Foreign Industrial Targeting and Its Effect on US Industries, Phase II:*, pp. 81–82.

38. Suomela, *et al., US International Trade Commission, Foreign Industrial Targeting and Its Effect on US Industries, Phase II:*, p. 82.

39. This section borrows liberally from Yuill and Allen, pp. 46–49 and 217–259.

40. See, for example, "Wirtschaftliche Bedeutung und Entwicklung Strukturschwacher Regionen." *Drucksache, 10/2629,* Deutscher Bundestag–10, Wahlperiode, 13 December 1984; and "Sicherung Vorhandener und Schaffung Neuer Arbeitsplätze Durch Eine Aktive Industriepolitik," *Drucksache,* 10/2630, Deutscher Bundestag–10, Wahlperiode, 13 December 1984.

41. After a long dispute, original hopes for a European Fighter Aircraft involving the UK, France, FRG, Italy, and Spain were dashed. See "Future of European Fighter Uncertain as Governments Fail to Agree," *Aviation Week and Space Technology,* June 3, 1985, pp. 119–122. By the summer of 1986 it appeared that two European aircraft projects would be competing; the European Fighter Aircraft (EFA) involving the above five countries minus France, and a French program aimed at producing a lighter weight military aircraft, designated Rafale. There is a chance that the Rafale project may be expanded to include the four European F-16 partner states of Belgium, the Netherlands, Denmark, and Norway. See "F-16 Follow-On: Five European Nations Consider Developing New Light Fighter," *Aviation Week and Space Technology,* January 27, 1986, pp. 18–19; and "Four Nations Seek Role in French Rafale Follow-on Program," *Aviation Week and Space Technology,* May 5, 1986, p. 26. In any event the Federal Republic of Germany is firmly in the EFA program which is to be headquartered, like the Tornado management group before it, in Munich. See "Four Nations Form Consortium to Develop European Fighter," *Aviation Week and Space Technology,* June 9, 1986, p. 28.

From the perspective of employment prospects in the West German aerospace industry, the important questions concern the volume and timing of production. Ideally, the new project should be phased in to absorb resources freed as production on the Tornado project runs down. Such a smooth transition is unlikely, given the delays normally associated with new multi-national projects. See, for example, "European Fighter Aircraft Falling Behind Schedule," *Aviation Week and Space Technology,* March 3, 1986, pp. 26–27. On the other hand, since the three principal partners have worked together in the management company Panavia for a decade on the Tornado project economies of experience may reduce somewhat the transaction cost of collaboration.

42. See "Arms Production: Everyone Has a Finger in the Pie," *Suddeutsche Zeitung,* Munich, February 9, 1985, translated in *The German Tribune,* February 24, 1985, p. 8.

43. "Arms Production: Everyone Has a Finger in the Pie," *Suddeutsche Zeitung.*

44. "Arms Production: Everyone Has a Finger in the Pie," *Suddeutsche Zeitung.*

45. See "New Liberal Arms Export Rules Force Review of German Policy," *Aviation Week and Space Technology,* December 2, 1985, pp. 27–28.

46. Howaldtwserke-Deutschewerft Aktiengesellschaft Hamburg und Kiel, *Annual Report and Accounts for the Financial Year 1982/83, October 1, 1982 to September 30, 1983,* pp. 9–13.

47. See "Shipbuilding: Jobs Threatened in Spite of Big Yard's Record Year," *Rheinischer Merkur/Christ und Welt,* Bonn, June 7, 1986, as translated in *The German Tribune,* July 13, 1986, p. 8. The truly desperate position of European shipbuilding has lead to a unified program by the Commission of European Economic Communities

designed to ameliorate the widespread distress. Grants to cover the cost of shipyard closures and welfare provisions to displaced workers, together with discouragement of capacity expansion, consititute the central elements of the EEC program. See "'Orderly Decline' Plan for Europe's Sinking Shipyards," *Stuttgarter Zeitung*, Stuttgart, October 20, 1986, as translated in *The German Tribune*, November 2, 1986, p. 8.

TABLE 4.1   Assistance to West German manufacturing as a share
of value added, by types of programs, 1974 (in %)

Industry	Domestic Subsidies			Effective Tariff Protection	Total
	Regional Programs	All Other	Total		
Stone and clay products	0.8	0.3	1.1	3.7	4.8
Basic iron and steel	0.4	0.2	0.6	17.0	17.6
Foundries	0.6	0.1	0.7	12.1	12.8
Rolling mills	0.5	0.1	0.6	7.7	8.3
Nonferrous metals	2.1	0.3	2.4	22.3	24.7
Chemicals	0.5	0.8	1.3	14.4	15.7
Saw mills	1.1	1.1	2.2	13.7	15.9
Pulp, paper, paperboard	0.7	0.2	0.9	29.6	30.5
Rubber and asbestos	0.5	0.1	0.6	8.7	9.3
Structural engineering	1.0	0.4	1.4	1.4	2.8
Machinery	0.5	0.8	1.3	2.5	3.8
Road motor vehicles	0.6	0.2	0.8	5.8	6.6
Aircraft	0.1	23.4	23.5	−0.9	22.6
Electrical equipment	1.9	0.8	2.7	4.5	7.2
Precision mechanics, optics, watches	0.9	0.8	1.7	4.9	6.6
Fabricated metal products	1.1	0.2	1.3	5.6	6.9
Precision ceramics, pottery	0.9	0.2	1.1	9.9	11.0
Glass	0.6	0.3	0.9	11.1	12.0
Woodworking	0.8	0.0	0.8	9.9	10.7
Musical instruments, toys	0.7	0.0	0.7	6.9	7.6
Paper products	0.6	0.2	0.8	19.9	20.7
Printing and publishing	0.6	3.8	4.4	5.3	9.7
Plastic products	1.1	0.2	1.3	9.8	11.1
Leather, leather goods, shoes	0.2	0.3	0.5	9.4	9.9
Textiles	0.7	0.6	1.3	20.8	22.1
Clothing	1.2	0.6	1.8	20.7	22.5

Source: H. H. Glismann and F. D. Weiss, "On the Political Economy of
Protection in West Germany," World Bank Staff Working Paper No. 427,
October 1980, p. 13, as cited in Suomela, et al., p. 70.

Table 4.2   WEST GERMANY: Development of the Financial Assistance of the State and of Tax Breaks, 1983-1986

	Financial Assistance or Tax Breaks – Millions of DM											
	1983 Actual			1984 Actual			1985 Estimated			1986 Projected		
		of that			of that			of that			of that	
CATEGORIES	Total	Financial Assistance	Tax Break	Total	Financial Assistance	Tax Break	Total	Financial Assistance	Tax Break	Total	Financial Assistance	Tax Break
	2	3	4	5	6	7	8	9	10	11	12	13
I. Food, Agriculture, Forestry	2,609	2,293	316	2,784	2,475	309	3,110	2,806	304	3,080	2,781	299
II. Business Activity (Excluding Transp.)												
1. Mining	1,354	1,230	124	2,032	1,913	119	1,628	1,506	122	1,279	1,157	122
2. Energy & Resources	433	317	116	408	270	138	437	288	149	447	283	164
3. Research & Development	786	576	210	852	551	301	1,034	722	312	1,128	805	323
4. Aid for Certain Industries												
– Shipbuilding	290	290	–	167	167	–	230	230	–	200	200	–
– Aerospace	243	243	–	309	309	–	670	670	–	491	491	–
– Steel	303	291	12	1,122	915	207	767	385	382	–	–	–
5. Regional Structural Measures	4,824	220	4,604	4,846	224	4,622	5,124	256	4,868	5,266	246	5,020
6. Other	1,362	309	1,053	1,648	327	1,321	1,712	373	1,339	1,706	352	1,354
TOTAL/SUMMARY – Part II	9,595	3,476	6,119	11,384	4,676	6,708	11,602	4,430	7,172	10,517	3,534	6,983

Financial Assistance or Tax Breaks – Millions of DM

CATEGORIES	1983 Actual — Total	Financial Assistance (of that)	Tax Break	1984 Actual — Total	Financial Assistance (of that)	Tax Break	1985 Estimated — Total	Financial Assistance (of that)	Tax Break	1986 Projected — Total	Financial Assistance (of that)	Tax Break
(column no.)	2	3	4	5	6	7	8	9	10	11	12	13
III. Transportation	1,888	1,028	860	1,819	970	849	1,813	847	871	1,896	1,000	896
IV. Housing — with } separation of mixed financing	-	-	-	-	-	-	7,764	4,232	3,532	7,867	4,276	3,591
without } mixed financing	6,140	3,347	2,793	6,777	3,561	3,216	7,482	3,950	3,532	7,585	3,994	3,591
V. Savings Incentives and Capital Formation — with } separation of mixed financing	-	-	-	-	-	-	3,439	2,060	1,379	3,190	1,870	1,320
without } mixed financing	4,185	2,869	1,316	3,249	1,918	1,331	2,909	1,530	1,379	2,660	1,340	1,320
VI. Other Tax Breaks	3,767	-	3,767	4,016	-	4,016	4,173	-	4,173	4,337	-	4,337
TOTAL/SUMMARY – I–VI — with } separation of mixed financing	-	-	-	-	-	-	31,906	14,475	17,431	30,887	13,461	17,426
without } mixed financing	28,184	13,013	15,171	30,029	13,600	16,429	31,094	13,663	17,431	30,075	12,649	17,426

NOTE: Income Equalization for Agriculture in the framework of decrease of currency Equalization of Value Added/Lump Sum Taxes (replacement of common market measures)

	1984 Actual	1985 Estimated	1986 Projected
Total	1,050	1,700	1,795
Gov't	1,600	2,600	2,700

SOURCE: 10th Subsidy Report, Overview Table #9.

5

Sweden

Swedish Industrial Policy[1]

Sweden maintains a market economy and government ownership in industry has traditionally been small. However, industrial expansion has always been the objective of general economic policy. Apparently this policy was successful in encouraging the very rapid industrial growth which occurred during the 1950s and 1960s. Government programs in the housing, communications, defense, and energy sectors contributed to this development.

The 1950s and 1960s were characterized by a significant structural transformation in the Swedish economy, with labor migrating from agriculture and forestry to industry and the service sector. The healthy demand for Swedish exports helped to ease the transition. An important element in the government's economic strategy was the use of general economic policy and labor market policies to aid the transfer of resources from less competitive sectors to more viable ones. The structural transformation was speeded up by the system of centralized wage agreements. Swedish dependence on foreign trade also expanded through a sharp growth of dependence on imported oil. At the same time, its industry became more internationally involved through increased direct investment abroad.

The positive overall economic development was, however, accompanied by a large decline in population in the northern parts of the country. This led to the introduction of a comprehensive regional policy in 1965 which was principally aimed at industry. It has played an important role in changing the industrial structure particularly in the northern parts of the country.

In the late 1960s, changes in the world economy together with other factors, influenced the competitive posture of Swedish industry. The concept of industrial policy which included a more active government role, was adopted and in 1969 the Ministry of Industry was established.

The 1973–1974 oil price increases, the subsequent prolonged worldwide recession, and growing competition from newly-industrializing countries, all had a strong effect on Swedish industry and on the direction of industrial policy. Certain traditionally important industries such as shipbuilding, iron and steel, and iron ore, were seriously hurt and support to such ailing industries became an important element of industrial policy. Aid to displaced workers and the affected communities also was viewed as necessary. In the late 1970s, government ownership of industry increased significantly as a result of the acquistion of companies in distress.

Counter to the experience in most other industrial states, industrial production in Sweden decreased slightly during the 1975–1982 period. Swedish industry suffered significant market share losses, capacity utilization and profitability dropped and the level of investment decreased.

Among the factors which contributed to this poor performance were the following:

- rapid cost increases in the mid-1970s;
- generally reduced world demand for investment goods;
- negative developments in certain sectors where Sweden had held a traditionally strong position;
- increased competition from newly industrializing countries; and
- inability to benefit from developments in new markets.

During 1983, the negative economic trends in Sweden were reversed. Industrial production increased by 5% over 1982 and the volume of exports climbed 10% over the prior year. The rate of decline in employment was reduced and capacity utilization and return on invested capital increased. This improvement was expected to continue through the next few years.

If inflation and production costs can be kept under control the longer-term industrial outlook for Sweden appears favorable. The painful structural adjustments of the last decade have resulted in a more competitive economy. Swedish industry is attempting to strengthen its long-term competitive position by investment in research and development and automation.

Industrial Policy Measures

The objective of Swedish policy has been to encourage the modernization of production and industrial expansion and renewal, but with a minimum of social disruption. Logically, industrial policy should be related to measures in other policy areas. The main objective of the government's economic policy is to facilitate a better utilization of Sweden's productive resources. Since roughly half of Sweden's industrial production is exported, the maintenance and strengthening of the multilateral free trade system has been an important Swedish goal. Also relevant are measures in the field of labor market policy which are designed to contribute to greater flexibility and to long-term adjustment between supply and demand in the labor market.[2] Educational policy also relates to long-term industrial development.

The state-owned industrial sector (excluding public utilities) accounts for roughly 7% of Swedish industrial production. A majority of the state-owned companies, distributed among several different industries, are found in the holding company Procordia AB.

As noted above, government support to ailing industries became an important element of industrial policy during the late 1970s. The net costs of industrial support measures increased from near 1 billion Swedish crowns (SKr) in fiscal year 1975–1976 to approximately SKr 17 billion in 1982–1983 in current prices. In fiscal year 1982–1983, non-permanent support that aimed at providing immediate relief to companies and sectors facing severe financial problems amounted to roughly SKr 12 billion.

A distinction is often made in Sweden between defensive support to ailing industries and more permanent, forward-looking and positive measures such as support to technical research and development, regional policy, promotion of small and medium-sized enterprises, export promotion, etc. During the period 1975–1982, roughly three-fourths of total government industrial support expenditure was of the former kind.

Ailing Industries. The government support measures taken during the 1975–1982 period were largely designed to help the Swedish mining, shipbuilding, forestry, iron, and steel industries adapt to new competitive conditions and to facilitate capacity reductions and resource transfers to more profitable and competitive sectors. Many of these measures were directed at state-owned companies.

Among the ailing industries, shipbuilding received the largest amount of aid. A long series of capacity reductions was initiated after the oil crisis in 1973–1974 when a dramatic decline in orders for new ships and rising international competition put severe strains on the Swedish shipbuilding industry. In 1977, all major Swedish shipyards were merged into a state-owned shipbuilding group, Svenska Varv AB (Swedyards). Since that time, Swedish shipbuilding capacity has been reduced by 75%. Three major shipyards have been closed and one has been wholly converted to the production of offshore drilling equipment. Employment in Swedish shipbuilding decreased from 31,000 in 1975 to about 14,800 in 1982. Swedyard's present structural plan anticipates further capacity reductions.

Problems confronting the steel industry also precipitated increased direct government involvement. SSAB-Svenskt Stal AB (with a current state ownership of 75%) was formed in 1978. Government aid has been extended intermittently to ease the company's financial difficulties and to facilitate structural changes which required closures and new investment. In the mid-1980s the company achieved profitability for the first time.

In 1979 serious financial problems led to government ownership of two firms in the forestry industry. Another already state-owned forest company, ASSI, also suffered heavy losses during the recession in the latter part of the 1970s and additional infusions of government funds were made.

During the latter part of the 1970s following a general decline in the European steel industry and emerging competition from overseas, the state-owned mining company in northern Sweden, LKAB, deteriorated sharply. Financial contributions were made in 1981 and early 1983. In connection with the latter decision, one of the company's mines in northern Sweden was taken out of operation.

Over the years, additional measures have been undertaken to support the textile and clothing industry. The decline in this sector has been particularly rapid due to high labor costs and increased imports. Imports account for around 80% of domestic consumption of clothing. Textile and clothing employment has fallen from 67,500 in 1970 to 30,000 in 1982.

Industrial R&D. Total R&D activity in Sweden amounted to 2.5% of GNP in 1983, with about two-thirds of it conducted by industry.

Support to technical research and development is administered by the National Board for Technical Development (Styrelsen För Teknisk Utveckling—STU). This body, which was established in 1968, is the central government agency charged with providing government support to technical research and development. It is primarily concerned with the development of projects up to the prototype (pilot) stage. Its support takes three forms. Grant aid is provided to universities and institutes and is primarily designed for support of pure research. An important condition for the receipt of such support is that the results be published and/or made widely available.

Support for cooperative research programs is available to encourage technical R&D of interest to an industry organization or to groups of firms. This aid is also provided as a grant, designed to offset about half of the costs of a specific program. Conditional loans are also used to encourage technical R&D and innovation in individual companies. Such loans are limited to the prototype phase of projects and usually cover up to 50% of project development costs. Loan payment is required only for successful projects.

The Swedish Industrial Development Fund.[3] The Swedish Industrial Development Fund (Industrifonden) was established by Parliament in 1979 with an initial capital of SKr 300 million. This was raised by SKr 450 million and in 1984 by another 600 million. Falling profits and an apparent scarcity of external risk capital together with high interest rates, motivated the establishment of the Fund as a new way of encouraging high-risk industrial projects by major Swedish firms with an existing position in international markets. The completion of large government investment programs in nuclear power and military aircraft also raised concerns about the future of strategically important firms. Against this background it is interesting to note that the Fund's two largest customers have been Volvo Flygmotor and Saab-Scania. In part this reflects the fact that the Fund has also been assigned the task of handling launch aid contracts between the government and the aerospace industry for aircraft and aeroengine projects. Such contracts alone amount to about SKr 650 million.

The Fund was given the task of supporting the development of new products, processes, and systems for industrial production. Its support may take the form of loans or other financial participation in larger projects. To be supported, projects must involve high risk, both technologically and commercially, but offer a high potential for profit. The maximum participation by the Fund is limited to 50% of project costs up to a maximum of SKr 50 million.

Credits require regular payments of interest and repayment when the level of risk has been reduced to a "normal" business level. In case of project failure, the Fund may give total or partial remission of debt. Participation can also take the form of a cash grant in return for a royalty in future revenues. In early 1983 a third form of support was permitted which resembles an indemnity, with the Fund paying part of project costs after it has become clear that the project has failed.

During its first four years of operation, projects in the transportation sector have received the largest financial support, with steel and metal ranking second. Instruments, pharmaceuticals, and electronics follow.

It would appear that the Industrifonden has taken over many of the functions of the Swedish National Development Company, Svenska Ut-vecklingsaktiebolaget (SUAB)[4] with the important exception that Industri-fonden does not hold ownership interest in the firms it supports. SUAB still exists as a combination of a development company and a staff function within the holding company for government-owned enterprises, described below. The Regional Development Funds administer a somewhat similar program for smaller and medium-sized companies which will be described below.

Space, Energy, and Microelectronics: The government feels that Sweden must stay abreast of space technology, and a program to enhance Swedish capabilities in this field was begun in 1979. The program includes Swedish participation in projects within the framework of the European Space Agency and national efforts such as the construction of the Viking scientific satellite and the Tele-X telecommunications satellite (in cooperation with Norway and Finland). Since 1975, considerable resources have been devoted to ambitious government-supported energy R&D programs with priority given to the development of energy-efficient industrial processes, heat storage, biomass for energy purposes, combustion technologies, and wind energy. The government believes that this program has had important industrial spin-offs.

In late 1983, the government proposed the establishment of a national program in the field of microelectronics in order to improve Swedish capabilities in this crucial field.

Industry-Specific Aid to Traditional Sectors. The National Industrial Board administers programs for certain traditional industries such as textiles and clothing, wood, and until mid-1984, the hand-made glass industry. The programs include consultancy services and various types of financial assistance designed to facilitate adjustment to structural change. Most of the financial support goes to the textile and clothing industry.

As in other maritime nations, Sweden has a support program for its shipbuilding industry. Write-off loans for Swedish shipyards subsidize production costs to improve the international competitiveness of Swedish shipyards and to offset subsidies granted to foreign shipyards. Subsidization of interest rates (in accordance with international agreements) also allows Swedish shipyards to remain competitive when favorable financing facilities are made available to competitors. Credit guarantees are also available for shipping companies.

Aid to Small and Medium-Sized Enterprises. A program to assist small firms (those employing fewer than 200 people) is administered jointly by the National Industrial Board, and the Regional Development Funds, which provide services and support, including loans, to small and medium-sized enterprises. There is a Regional Development Fund in each of Sweden's 24 counties.

The aim of the development capital support program of Regional Development Funds is the promotion of new products, new markets, and other developments in small firms—mainly manufacturing firms and companies that provide services to industry. The aid, frequently combined with the provision of advice, takes the form of a conditional loan or a conditional grant, each repayable if the project is successful. The Regional Development Funds may also issue loan guarantees to small and medium-sized companies. The Funds may provide loans both for working assets and for investments. The maximum amount available for such a loan is SKr 2 million per company. The Regional funds may also provide capital for development projects up to SKr 3 million per company.

General industry loan guarantees are also available. These guarantees are virtually identical to those issued by the Regional Development Funds, but they are also available to firms employing more than 200 people. In addition, measures are available to encourage the development of small and medium-sized enterprises by the promotion of trading in the shares of such companies, and of venture capital firms.

Export Promotion. In 1972, the government and the privately-owned General Swedish Export Association formed the Swedish Trade Council. The government provides its budget but companies that subscribe to its services pay a fee. The role of the Trade Council is to plan and implement measures aimed at promoting Swedish exports. The council is assisted by a number of Swedish Trade Offices abroad.

In addition, Sweden has a system of state-supported export credits and export credit guarantees. Medium and long-term export credits can be refinanced by the Swedish Export Credit Corporation (a financial institution owned jointly by the government and commercial banks) at subsidized interest rates based on the OECD Arrangement on Guidelines for Officially Supported Export Credits. Export credit guarantees are issued by the Export Credit Guarantee Board.

Regional Policy Measures.[5] Sweden is a fairly large country (almost the area of France) but with a small popluation—just over 8.3 million. The population is unevenly distributed and concentrated in the southern parts of the country. Such regional imbalances were aggravated as a result of the rapid structural change in the Swedish economy during the 1960s. As a result, a comprehensive regional policy was introduced in 1965. The objective of regional policy is to stabilize population in different parts of the country and provide access to jobs, services, and a good environment throughout the country.

Sweden has a considerable number of regional aids many of which are rarely found elsewhere in Europe and/or have unique features. There are, for example, transfer grants to compensate key personnel for the cost of moving with new firms going to the assisted areas. In 1983, a new measure was introduced which allows a concession on social security charges in Norrbotten county which holds some 3% of the national population. The basic concession involves a reduction of social security charges by ten percentage points, at a cost of some SKr 330 million annually. Elsewhere in Sweden's assisted areas there are three main incentives—location loans, location grants, and employment grants.

The location loan is a discretionary, project-related loan. Interest rates are above the official Swedish discount rate (currently, by 4.25 percentage points) but, at the discretion of the authorities, interest and/or principal repayment holidays can be awarded for up to 5 years. Location loans are available to firms located anywhere in the Swedish assisted areas—areas which currently hold some 13.5% of the Swedish national population, following a major cutback (from 28.6% of the population) in July 1982. The new assisted areas divide into three categories—ranging from Area A (the worst-off area) down to Area C (the most prosperous of the assisted areas).

Location grants are normally awarded in conjunction with a location loan. The location grant is a discretionary, project-related capital grant— up to 50% of eligible investment in Area A, 35% in Area B, and 20% in Area C—subject to overt subsidy cost-per-job limits (SKr 450,000 in Area A, SKr 350,000 in Area B, SKr 200,000 in Area C). Location grants and location loans (and other State aids) cannot, in combination, exceed 70% of eligible investment. The award of a location grant is conditional on job and other targets being fulfilled. If agreed targets are not met, location grants can be "reclaimed" by the authorities by being converted into a location loan. Such powers of reclaim diminish over time with the entire grant "non-reclaimable" after seven years.

Finally, the employment grant, an incentive type rare in Europe, takes the form of a fixed sum paid annually for up to seven years in return for additional labor hired by firms located in the designated problem areas (Areas A, B, and C). The rate of award and its duration are determined by the location of the firm; and range from SKr 55,000 per additional employee (paid over a three-year period) up to SKr 180,000 per additional employee (paid over a seven-year period).

A somewhat different form of regional aid exists which is managed by a publicly-owned foundation; Industricentra. It has built industrial estates (parks) in strategically located towns important for industrial development and leased them to privately owned manufacturing firms at subsidized rents.

Industrial Policy Reorientation. The return to power of a socialist government in October 1982 brought a number of measures designed to reverse the period of industrial decline. While the most visible decision was the 16% devaluation of the Swedish crown, this move was supplemented with special programs to increase investment in energy, transport and housing, with special measures in the field of labor market policy.

In the budget bill presented in January 1983 the government stated that while support to ailing industries might bring short-term advantages, such measures often delay necessary structural adjustment. The government has also acknowledged that reduced industrial subsidies would be necessary to help in reducing the budget deficit.

Recent Changes in Industrial Policy. The Swedish Parliament has recently approved an agreement between Sweden and Norway for cooperation in telecommunication satellites. Finland will also participate in the first project under this agreement—the launching of the Tele-X satellite.

In late 1983, the government proposed measures aimed at coordinating activities in the field of marine offshore technology. A national program was also established to encourage work in the field of microelectronics. The decision in early 1983 to proceed with the JAS-39 Gripen military aircraft project was a highly significant one for the future of the Swedish aerospace industry.

The reoriented industrial policy also appears to be attempting to identify such possiblities for expansion as may exist in the traditional raw material-based industries. Thus, measures have been taken to secure the supply of raw materials for the forest industry, to expand minerals exploration, and to establish a more competitive structure for the specialty steel industry.

Following a government recommendation in early 1983, the National Swedish Industrial Board has been assigned new functions as the central government agency for industrial policy and regional policy aid for the business sector. Important measures have been implemented in the field of energy investment and energy technology development.

Generally, a shift in the pattern of government assistance to industry is observable with a significant decrease in expenditure for defensive support measures. During fiscal year 1983–1984 such expenditures declined to SKr 3.5 billion, from the 1982–1983 level of 12 billion.

Measures Proposed in the 1984 Bill. The industrial policy bill presented by the government in March 1984 stressed the importance of positive action rather than continuing support to ailing industries. While the government has not abandoned such industries, it stressed that continued aid to traditional sectors must be carefully designed to strengthen their ability to compete in current international markets. Government statements also emphasize that future industrial policy measures should focus on the development of efficient and promising activities. It also appears willing to consider the possibility of bankruptcy more seriously when dealing with companies in substantial commercial difficulties. In part, this reflects the recognition that the maintenance of employment in ailing industries through subsidies can be unacceptably expensive.

The bill on industrial expansion and renewal was accompanied by a bill on research policy which effects the activities of the National Board for Technical Development (STU). It was proposed that SKr 200 million be allocated to the Board during the three-year period 1984–1985 to 1986–1987. Increased priority is to be given to financial support for small high-technology companies and to aid individual innovators.

The bill on industrial expansion and renewal included proposals concerning priorities and financing of the national microelectronics program during fiscal years 1984–1985 to 1986–1987. It emphasized the importance of the information technology sector and the potential that exists there for Swedish industry. In addition, the bill presented proposals to utilize government procurement as a means of furthering technological development.

It also outlined a three-year program for the National Industrial Board including support for the development of technology-intensive small and medium-sized enterprises. The Board was also assigned other tasks related to the encouragement of small and medium-sized industry. Further, a special fund for small and medium-sized enterprises was established. The purpose of the fund, which is affiliated with the Swedish Investment Bank, is to ease the difficulties encountered in financing such enterprises.

The State-Owned Industrial Sector. In early 1983, a decision was taken to reorganize the state holding company, Statsföretag AB (recently renamed Procordia AB). Certain important raw materials-based companies (the mining company, LKAB; the forest company, ASSI; and the steel company, SSAB; as well as Swedish Petroleum) were taken over directly by the State. While government ownership in industry increased signficantly during the latter part of the 1970s, in the early 1980s the State sold companies in the electronics field (Datasaab and Luxor) and the nuclear engineering company (Asea-Atom) to private industry.

New objectives and principles for the operation of state-owned enterprises were promulgated by the Parliament in early 1983. Thus, the objective of Procordia now is to run a profitable business and to increase efficiency, competitiveness and possibilities for expansion. If a state-owned company is requested by the government to undertake a task which does not flow from its normal commercial operations (for regional policy reasons, for example) it may expect to receive compensation from the government. The basic goal is that Procordia ultimately should manage itself without any support from the government. A fundamental unanswered question to a foreign observer is why government ownership is deemed necessary to restore such companies to profitability.

Labor Market Policy.[6] Labor market policy is designed to aid in the process of job placement and includes selective measures to improve opportunities for those in the labor force to locate and keep their jobs. These tasks are the responsibility of the National Labor Market Administration. The Adminstration depends upon the Labor Market Board (Arbetsmarknadsstyrelesen, AMS), the central administrative agency for general labor market matters which directly supervises the county labor boards and employment service offices. The employment service theoretically is responsible for all job placement in the country since private employment agencies are prohibited by law. Backing this function of the employment service is a law which requires that almost all job vacancies be registered at the local employment service office. However, firms are not required to hire all referrals from the service and may do their own recruiting without involving the service. Also of interest is the fact that representatives of management organizations and trade unions are actively involved at every level (and in every function) of the Labor Market Administration. Swedish labor market policy has expanded substantially since the late 1950s, largely reflecting the influence of the trade union economist Gösta Rehn.[7] The underlying philosophy was that a policy goal of attaining full employment primarily through expansionary monetary and fiscal policies bore a high risk of inflation and that more restrained macro-policies implemented together with ambitious and selective labor market measures would be more successful.

During the rapid economic expansion and structural transformation of Swedish industry in the 1960s the primary goal was to encourage and facilitate geographical and occupational mobility. However, the structural shifts during that decade contributed to the creation of social welfare problems and growing regional imbalance which, in the late 1960s, nudged labor market policy in the direction of regional development and aid to persons with occupational handicaps.

During the 1970s a subtle transformation occurred which replaced the "full employment" goal with one of "work for everyone." The latter focused upon the entry into the labor market of types of persons previously viewed as outside the work force and greater equality between the sexes. Quality of life at the work place was also stressed with emphasis upon "the intrinsic value of work as a means of creating a sense of community."[8]

Measures to Increase the Demand for Labor. In the severe recession of the late 1970s Swedish labor market policy operated within the firm with various subsidies paid to employers to keep people within jobs until general economic conditions improved. The largest was for stockpiling. Thus, in 1972 and 1975, 1977 firms faced with declining demand received inventory maintenance grants as an incentive to maintain output and employment.

Employment subsidies were introduced in 1977 for companies in sensitive job market sectors; namely employing elderly workers in the textile and clothing industries and companies in a dominant position in a local labor market. Recruitment grants were added in 1978–1979. These were temporary subsidies designed to encourage firms to speed up their recruitment of new employees during the economic recovery then under way. A similar subsidy known as a temporary employment grant was made available in 1981–1982. In addition, the grant to firms in a dominant labor market position was replaced by a similar subsidy called a readjustment grant. It is equal to 75% of the total wage and salary costs of employees who have been given notice of dismissal and is payable for up to 6 months. A worker who finds a new job after receiving notice is permitted to keep half of his/her previous wage during the remainder of the grant period in addition to the pay of the new job. This is seen as an incentive for employees who have been given notice to seek new work.

In view of its special economic significance, the construction industry receives special attention. A planning system for construction activity has been introduced which is based on collaboration among labor, management, local governments, and the Labor Market Administration. While voluntary, this collaboration takes place under the auspices of regional construction work committees which recommend starting dates for various projects from a seasonal standpoint designed to stabilize construction industry employment. Starting dates for lower priority construction projects can be postponed for more than one year, depending on seasonal and cyclical influences.

Finally, a major tool designed to prevent layoffs or dismissals consists of paying subsidies to firms that sponsor training courses for their employees instead of cutting back employment. Training grants are also available for other purposes such as the encouragement or hiring in regions of weak employment and the training of the elderly or disabled.

The above measures are all aimed at increasing the demand for labor at the level of the firm. In addition, policies exist which are designed to enhance demand through their impact on the individual. The first of these consists of relief work projects for the unemployed. While traditionally such jobs have been in construction and civil engineering projects, since the mid-1970s, relief jobs for young people have been concentrated in local government services and the health care sector. In 1981–1982, 59% of those on relief work were young people in the 18 to 24 year age bracket. Beginning in January 1982, relief work openings were created for 16- and 17-year-olds also. While relief jobs are paid generally at regular labor market rates, the 16- and 17-year-olds receive Skr 85 per day of which 75 is a grant from the National Board of Education. The shift in the nature of relief jobs for youth reflects in part a desire to engage them in public service activities which are of clear aid to other people and which might provide a useful foundation for subsequent choice of occupation or continued education.

At the other end of the age spectrum are the "adjustment groups" whose purpose is to prevent less competitive persons (older and/or disabled) from being forced out of the labor market while also improving the chances that such persons will be hired. Employment service offices focus their efforts in this program on firms recruiting new employees. Several laws were passed in the 1970s, both to reinforce job security of those already employed and to aid the employment services in finding jobs for hard-to-place persons seeking employment.

The Act on Security of Employment requires employers to give legally acceptable reasons for firing workers and to provide a notice period ranging from one to six months, depending on the age of the worker. Those dimissed for lack of work in the company also must receive right of first refusal if the company later hires new employees.

The Act Concerning Certain Employment-Promoting Measures requires advance notice of from two to six months to county labor boards in the event of cutbacks in production. It also gives labor market authorities the option of wide-ranging negotiations with firms designed to further the hiring of hard-to-place persons seeking employment. Employment with subsidized pay is also available to enlarge the demand for occupationally handicapped people.

Measures to Influence the Supply of Labor. Perhaps the most important of these measures is the subsidization of geographical mobility. The employment service can provide financial aid, as well as perform job-placement functions. Such aid can cover actual moving expenses, starting grants, and per diem allowances covering the temporary extra costs of double residency.

Also, significant in shaping the available labor supply is labor market training to meet individual requirements. Such training (outside the firm) is designed to help the unemployed and hard-to-place job seekers who require occupational skills. In addition, there is "bottleneck training" for persons who are employed and not in danger of job loss. Here the objective is to increase the supply of skills that are in short supply. Most of these training activities are provided as special courses financed by the National Board of Education and are conducted at labor market training centers or in upper secondary schools. Although most such courses are vocationally oriented, there are also some preparatory courses, readjustment and training courses, and Swedish language courses for immigrants.

Labor market training is free to participants and those aged 20 and above receive training grants ranging from SKr 165 to 280 per day. Teenagers without dependents receive a daily allowance of SKr 100. In 1982, the average daily pay of industrial workers was about SKr 300. Individually-oriented training grew rapidly during the 1970s and in fiscal 1981–1982, about 90,000 persons participated of whom 43% were women. Follow-up studies indicate that most of those who begin labor market training actually complete it and 60 to 70% of students in the specially arranged vocational training courses found jobs in the labor market within six months of completing their programs.

Matching Activities. Perhaps the most traditional function of Swedish labor market policy is that of matching job seekers with job vacancies. Even here however, the public employment service offers a wide array of assistance measures to the job seeker beyond referral to a potential employer. In addition to actual job placement, Swedish matching activities include vocational counseling and training, aptitude testing, occupational rehabilitation and placement in employment outside the regular labor market (relief work, employment with subsidized pay, or sheltered workshop employment).

Swedish unemployment rates have traditionally been low relative to other industrialized nations. For example, during the 1970s annual averages fluctuated between 1.5% and 2.7% of the labor force. During the 1980–1982 period registered unemployment reached its highest post-World War II levels averaging 3.1% in 1982. Most Western European and North American observers would be envious of a rate that low which, for Sweden, is a high. It is of course not scientifically demonstrable that Swedish success here is a consequence of its labor market policies but one is tempted to conclude that they must have been doing something right. These accomplishments occurred despite three major recessions (1971–1973, 1976–1978, and 1981–1983), a substantial increase in the labor force participation of women, and structural declines in the Swedish forestry, shipbuilding, and basic steel industries.[9]

Swedish Interest
in Economic Conversion and Disarmament

Sweden is probably unique among advanced industrial states in its intense and continuing interest in economic conversion and disarmament. For well over a century it has been able to maintain a position of neutrality. This has resulted from the exercise of a cautious foreign policy, the maintenance of respectable military power, and luck. The absence of recent imperialist pretensions with associated colonial interests or treaty obligations in distant corners of the world have permitted the Swedes to focus their strategy on protecting the homeland. Thus, Swedish military expenditures reflect the Swedish perception of the east-west conflict and the respect shown for its territorial integrity by its neighbors.

The nation's highly developed sense of community and concern for the social welfare of its citizens has made the trade-off between civil and military expenditures particularly obvious and painful. One result of these pressures has been the appearance of a series of official government studies and reports dealing with economic and social consequences of conversion and disarmament. The titles and principal findings and recommendations of some of these follow:[10]

Industridepartementet, Civil Produktion I Försvarsindustrin Betänkande Fran Försvarsindustrikommitten (Civil Production in the Defense Industry: Report of the Defense Industry Committee) Ds I 1982: 1 The committee inquired into methods available to assist defense firms to increase their output of civilian goods should the volume of government orders for defense products fall below the level necessary to sustain current production. The study concluded that resource transfer would be possible to meet public sector demand, particularly in the areas of energy, environmental protection, communications, and health.

Recommendations included the establishment of local working groups within each defense firm to stimulate and coordinate civil sector production and an interdepartmental working group to coordinate the efforts of the various government ministries. The Committee also suggested a state subsidy for civil projects to be financed by a surcharge on all defense procurement contracts awarded by the Defence Materiel Administration (Försvarets Materielverk, FMV). A surcharge of 0.5% of the contract value awarded in 1980–1981 would have yielded SKr 30.2 million ($5.5 million in 1981 prices) to be used by defense contractors to develop civil products.

Industridepartementet, Civil Produktion I Försvarsindustrin Genom Tekni-kupphandling (Civil Production in the Defense Industry Through Technology Procurement. Report by the Defense Industry Committee) Ds I 1983: 1 This continuation of the Defense Industry Committee's work inquired into how the procurement of technology by the government from the civil sector could be increased. The Committee concluded that coordination of procurement requirements of the various social sectors and the promotion and funding of large development projects were necessary if civil sector technology procurement was to help shift the orientation of production by defense firms. The report also recommended that state subsidies be provided to fund development work in the civil sector.

Flygindustridelegationens Betänkande (Report of the Aerospace Industry Delegation) Ds I 1980: 2 This inquiry examined how resources of the Swedish aerospace industry which have been utilized for military purposes could be put to civil use if and when a decline in government military orders occurs. The report identified the widely differing marketing methods involved in military and civil sales as a major obstacle to the conversion of the aerospace industry to civilian markets. Its authors also identified such obvious alternative fields as civil aircraft and space activities as requiring development programs similar to those found in military aerospace. Easing the transition with government-provided aid (loans and subsidies) was recommended.

Framtida Militär Flygindustri I Sverige. Principbetänkande Av 1979 Års Militara Flygindustrikommitte (Sweden's Military Aerospace Industry in the Future: Main Report of the 1979 Military Aerospace Industry Committee) Ds Fö 1981: 2 The Aerospace Industry Committee analyzed the impact of alternative approaches to the procurement of a successor to the Viggen military aircraft on the future structure of the Swedish aerospace sector. These alternatives included "off-the-shelf" purchase of a foreign aircraft, domestic assembly of a foreign-designed aircraft, or domestic design and production. The last alternative was selected as the preferred method to secure the aircraft-designated JAS-39 Gripen. It was argued that this approach would be most consistent with the development of an expanding civilian sector market for Swedish aerospace. While this goal was being pursued, ostensibly work on the military aircraft would enhance the industry's technical competence and keep its plant and equipment busy. The committee felt that this latest interlude of military involvement would provide an opportunity for the industry to seriously consider how it might reduce its dependence on the military market.

In addition, at least two other documents examine several aspects of the problem but unfortunately no summaries are available in English. These are: *Försvarets Forskningsanstalt, Svensk Försvarsindustri: Struktur, Kompetens, Utvecklingsbetingelser, FOA Rapport, C 10200-M5, Februari, 1982* (Defense Ministry, Swedish Defense Industry: Structure, Competence, Conditions of Development); and *Defense Ministry, Försvarsindustriella Problem, 1975–11–13,* (Defense Industrial Problems).

Most recently, Inga Thorsson, former Under-Secretary of State in the Swedish Foreign Ministry and head of the Swedish Disarmament Delegation in Geneva, published a report entitled, *In Pursuit of Disarmament: Conversion from Military to Civil Production in Sweden,* Volume 1A, *Background, Facts, Analyses;* and Volume 1B, *Summary, Appraisals, Recommendations.* (Stockholm: Liber Allmänna Förlaget, 1984). This two-volume study was conducted in response to a recommendation for such country case studies by the Group of 27 Governmental Experts at the United Nations (UN) which produced the *Report on the Relationship between Disarmament and Development* in 1982. This group was also chaired by Mrs. Thorsson.

While the background section is heavily laden with ideological baggage, the analytical portions of this study provide an interesting and useful description of the Swedish defense sector, and its impact on the Swedish economy.

The impact analysis is based on the assumption that by the year 2015, NATO and the Warsaw Treaty Organization will have reduced the size of their armed forces by 50% under terms of agreements likely to be signed over the next 10 or 15 years.[11] Two scenarios are developed from this assumption. In one, the armed forces of the two alliances would, as a whole, be cut in half but clearly offensive units would be cut even more. In the second, there would be an across the board reduction of 50% in conventional forces. The analysis assumes that under the first scenario Sweden would be able to reduce its military defense by 50% and by 40% under the second. The total resulting savings over the 1990–2015 period would vary between SKr 120 and 150 billion ($15 to 19 billion) in 1984 prices. The report correctly points out that such an amount would not automatically be available for redistribution due to unknown "future developments and the priorities of future governments."[12] The macroeconomic impacts of such a reduction are estimated to be quite small and certainly manageable. The analysis suggests a total loss of jobs over the 25-year period within the armed forces and the defense industrial sector of about 34,000. When the labor implications are viewed dynamically as a flow including both recruitment and retirement, this translates into 1,430 people leaving jobs in the defense sector annually or under 1% of the Swedish labor force.[13]

The authors of the report stress that although the likely economic consequences of such an appreciable reduction in military spending would be modest, "other factors play a decisive role." Disarmament is seen as "a political process which must be strongly supported by the entire population and backed up by a firm political will if it is to succeed. Disarmament must not be prevented or slowed down due to fears that it will produce unemployment or other serious difficulties."[14] Continuing, "Defence-sector employees should not experience disarmament as a threat to their future. The promotion of detente, peace and a reduction in defence expenditure must not be allowed to be retarded either in Sweden or in any other country because of concern for increased unemployment."[15] It is this strong belief that disarmament is too important to be derailed by perhaps misguided fears of its economic consequences that leads the authors to stess continuous monitoring by the government of defense-dependent regions and communities and a forceful and organized government role in support of the conversion process. The contrast between this position and that of the West German government noted earlier couldn't be more profound.

The report stesses that the successful transfer of resources currently utilized in the defense sector to civilian uses "without violating the objectives of defence policy" will be in the interest of all Swedish society and that since the defense sector has developed such a large dependence on government contracts, "Society therefore has a relatively larger responsiblity for what happens to defence industry employees."[16] Again, "The government has a special responsibility to see that . . . diversification occurs."[17] The authors foresee an active role for the government in such a conversion effort and refer to "Government-supported and co-ordinated programmes."[18]

Against this background of analysis and value judgments, the authors propose several policy recommendations to the government:[19]

- the establishment of a Council for Disarmament and Conversion;
- the creation of a central conversion fund to be administered by the Council; and
- the setting up of local conversion funds within each defense firm.

The council would include representatives of the Cabinet Office of the Prime Minister, the Ministries of Foreign Affairs, Defense, Labor, and Industry. Others on the Council are to be delegates from such interested agencies as the Defense Materiel Administration, the National Industrial Board, the National Labor Market Board, and the Board for Technical Development. In addition, representatives would include those from local authorities, trade and industry, and central trade union organizations. The activities of the Council would be administered by a small secretariat, lodged in the Cabinet Office of the Prime Minister.

The Council would undertake the following tasks:

- monitor developments in the armed forces and the defense sector, particularly in areas especially dependent on military spending;
- closely follow military spending, arms production and trade, conversion projects, etc.;
- explore ways to expand employment in civilian production among defense producers;
- work with defense firms and unions to apply existing industrial, regional, and employment policies to aid in the conversion issue; and
- administer the central conversion fund to encourage civil sector output within the defense industry and research designed to better understand the conversion process.

The authors proposed that the central conversion fund be of a sizeable amount, perhaps SKr 100 million ($12.5 million) and become effective on January 1, 1986, 6 months after the recommended date for the establishment of the Council.

Before disarmament begins (whose savings ostensibly could finance the Conversion Fund) several alternative methods of funding these activities might be considered. The authors identify the following: a surcharge on FMV (Defense Materiel Board) payments to defense firms financed by the budget of the Defense Ministry; the use of funds already in the budget to promote employment policies; and the imposition of a special tax on the export of war materiel. Mrs. Thorsson prefers the last alternative as possessing "considerable budgetary, political, and economic advantages over the others."[20] A figure of 5% on defense-related exports is recommended to take effect in the fiscal year 1985–1986.

A distinction should be made here between what the Swedish government considers military equipment not classified as war materiel, i.e., essentially dual purpose equipment sold for civilian use (unarmed tracked vehicles and patrol boats, radio-communication equipment, etc.), and war materiel per se. The proposed levy would not be imposed on such equipment designed for civilian usage. The export of such items is also subject to less stringent rules than that of weapons.

The authors recognize that one obvious response to a decline in domestic purchases of military equipment would be to attempt to increase exports of such weaponry. They clearly disapprove of such an adjustment on moral grounds and argue furthermore that increased arms exports do not constitute a long term solution because, ". . . in a period of disarmament there would be considerable competition for export markets among the major producing countries."[21] This may overstate the likely shrinkage of the market demand for arms in the non-industrialized world since many of the conflicts which rage there are largely independent of the East-West competition. It is likely, however, that increased competition for export markets would be a consequence of a substantial disarmament in Europe and North America.

The local conversion funds that the report's authors recommend be established within each defense firm might be used to expand civil activities. These funds could come from a state conversion supplement of perhaps 1% of the value of contracts placed by the Defense Materiel Administration (FMV). The authors suggest that a condition for the receipt of such support be the matching of its level with funds contributed by the defense contractors themselves.[22] Presumably such local conversion funds would be jointly administered by defense firm management and union officials.

The authors have no illusions that the Swedish model which they have recommended would be particularly suited to meet the challenges of defense industry conversion among the superpowers or in other countries with large defense sectors. They do feel, however, that if Sweden can demonstrate that a smooth transition is possible with minimal dislocation and modest financial outlay this will ". . . broaden international support for disarmament."[23] Any embarrassing shortfall in aggregate demand might be compensated by generous contributions to a UN International Disarmament Fund for Development.[24]

Reactions to the Thorsson Report

At the time of this writing the Thorsson report is just that—a study and recommendations by Mrs. Thorsson, a distinguished peace activist and retired ambassador, and her secretariat. At the time of the field work in Stockholm, the document had been widely disseminated to a variety of groups, public and private, for their reactions. Until such responses have been submitted and considered by the government, the document does not represent Swedish government policy. This point was made repeatedly by government officials. A common theme was that while the government is clearly interested in the issue of conversion as such, not all officials of the government were prepared to accept the recommendations of the report. For example, it was noted that while a small office to study conversion issues might be useful, there was not unanimous support for its establishment as a major and formal appendage of the office of the Prime Minister. The distinct impression given was that a small, competently staffed office for conversion analysis might be useful and, certainly, "there was no harm in it." Other government officials expressed agreement with the analytical portions of the report but found the disarmament scenarios unrealistic and tantamount to unilateral Swedish disarmament, something which I was assured no serious observer expects to occur.

Executives of defense firms were not supportive of the idea that the work of the Council for Disarmament and Conversion be financed by a 5% charge against military exports. Some found this recommendation a confirmation of their suspicion that the report is simply the latest political statement of the Swedish "peace movement" which views military spending and military exports as essentially evil.

Apparently the report was received more warmly by several Swedish trade union organizations which have long supported conversion planning as an essential step in breaking the link between military spending and fear of job loss among workers.[25] Dramatic evidence of the existence of such fear is found in the term given to teams of government officials who visit Swedish communities to study the possibility of military base closings—"death squads." One government official stressed that the closure of military bases requiring the adjustment of certain municipalities and regions may present a more serious problem than changing levels of orders for military equipment. In his view certain geographical areas were more dependent on military spending than most supplier firms and also had less experience with the process of "continuous rationalization."

An underlying source of divergent opinions concerning the Thorsson report appears to be the view of observers concerning variations in military spending. Those who see the modern industrial state as uniquely dependent on military spending are inclined to see substantial shifts in military procurement as a challenge to the basic structure of the economic and social order clearly requiring special planning, monitoring, and attention. Others who see variations in military spending as cyclical are inclined to view the phenomenon as less unique and as another variation which managers in a dynamic economy must learn to accommodate. Reasonable advance notice and familiar instruments of economic policy—macro and micro—are seen as adequate to the task of relatively smooth transition. Some holding the latter view cite Swedish experience with economic conversion in the past. A government official noted that economic conversion occurred successfully in the late 1960s and 1970s when economic and technological developments forced entire branches of Swedish industry to restructure their units for economic survival.

Attitudes Toward Industrial Diversification

Adjustment to changing market conditions often is approached as a problem which requires firms to diversify their product lines. Of interest were the responses of industrialists who cautioned against excessive diversification. Thus, a Saab Aircraft Division executive related how after investing substantial sums of money in new product development (wind energy mechanisms, un-manned submarines, electronics, and space products), the company concluded that the division's comparative advantage was in aircraft and that was where they would concentrate its principal operations. As he put it, "We are trained for large, high-technology projects requiring sheet metal working and to change that is almost impossible." Saab concluded that its aircraft division should focus on aircraft proper and all other high technology spinoff products derived from military aircraft operations were sorted out and put into a new company, Combitech, wholly owned by Saab.[26]

Claes-Ulrik Winberg, then President of the Bofors Group, [now known as Nobel Industries after merging with Kema Nobel in 1984], in discussing the restructuring of the company in his Annual Report for 1983, observed that operations have been grouped within four fields (chemistry, plastics, electronics, and biotechnics), all of which have a technical, technological and/or commercial link to the firm's core operations in ordinance.[27] Again the focus is to remain within areas logically related to what the company does best.

Changing Dependence on Defense Production. Table 5.1 illustrates the degree of defense dependency of sales and employment of nine of Sweden's principal defense producers in 1983. Among substantial size organizations, FFV (Förenade Fabriksverken-the National Defense Factories Group) and the Bofors Group lead with approximately 70% and 50%, respectively, of total sales going to the military. Beyond these, the military shares decline, especially at the corporate and/or group level. This is illustrated most dramatically in the case of Saab-Scania. While this firm is the largest supplier of defense equipment to the Swedish military, accounting for almost 25% of all purchases of equipment and R&D by the armed forces in 1982–1983, its military dependence at the corporate level was only 8% of sales and about 14% of domestic employment. On the other hand, Saab's aircraft division was overwhelmingly devoted to the military market while about half of the sales and employment of the Combitech division were dependent on the military customer. A similar pattern is seen in the wide disparity between degree of military dependence between Volvo at the corporate level (very small) and Volvo Flygmotor (appreciable). In the remaining five cases, the firms in the table are, in effect, the military offsprings of more diversified corporate parents.

Some of these offsprings have impressive records of reducing their degree of military dependence. Thus, for example, Volvo Flygmotor has moved into work on drive systems, heater products, diesel engine components, and hydraulics in addition to collaboration on civil aeroengines with Garrett,

General Electric, and Pratt and Whitney of the United States. The company has positioned itself across the full sprectrum of aircraft engine size with these collaborations. Thus the Garrett TFE 731-5 and TPE 331-14/15 engines are under 10,000 pounds of thrust for use in corporate aircraft and light passenger planes; the Pratt and Whitney JT8D-200 is in the 20,000-30,000 pounds of thrust range for medium-sized passenger aircraft of the DC-9 class; and the G.E. CF6-80A and CF6-80C are in the 50,000-60,000 pounds of thrust class for large wide-body and stretch aircraft. Approximately 40% of the cost of each new engine program was funded by the Swedish government with repayment on a royalty basis expected if the projects are commercially successful. Volvo Flygmotor executives believe that the market for the Pratt and Whitney JT8D-200 engine will turn out to be much larger than originally anticipated and that the government will find its investment in this project quite profitable. It has set a goal of reducing its military sales to about one-third of its total in 1990, an impressive reduction from approximately 90% military in 1970.

As noted in Table 5.1, the dependence on the military market, both in terms of sales and employment, of Saab-Scania's Aircraft division is very high. It is interesting to note that directly after World War II Saab attempted to develop civil aircraft and actually produced a 30-seat propeller-driven plane. Only a few had been produced when the Korean War erupted and the Swedish government ordered Saab to return to military work. A license to produce the passenger aircraft was given to Fokker in the Netherlands. Saab focused on military aircraft for the following three decades and there was a continuous development of such aircraft through the 1960s. The current front line Viggen series was developed in the 1960s and production will continue through the 1980s.

A major debate began in the early 1970s as to whether there should be a Swedish developed and produced successor to the Viggen in view of the high costs associated with such a project. There was strong pressure to buy a foreign aircraft which would be modified for Swedish defense needs. This scenario was not particularly attractive to Saab, and in 1977 the Board of Directors set the goal of achieving a 50-50 split between military and civil aircraft before the end of the 1980s. A major search for civil aircraft projects was undertaken and the Saab aircraft division is now engaged in five civil projects:

- the production of parts (flaps and vanes) as subcontractor for the McDonnell-Douglas DC-9 and of carbon graphite wing spoilers for the successor MD-80;
- general engineering work in Douglas Aircraft Division's propfan aircraft development program;
- participation in the initial development of the 7J7 with Boeing and possible design and production of selected portions of the aircraft.[28];
- the production of parts of the empenage and wing for the British Aerospace BAe 146 transport, also as subcontractor, and;

• the joint development, production, and marketing with Fairchild Industries of the US of a twin-turboprop regional airliner and corporate aircraft, the Saab-Fairchild 340, now in production.[29]

The JAS-39 Gripen Project

Serial production of the Viggen aircraft is expected to continue through 1988 with production of the new JAS-39 Gripen to begin thereafter with the first deliveries expected in 1992.[30] The Gripen will resemble the Viggen with its double delta, canard wing design. This provides the high lift necessary for the short take-off and landing (STOL) operational mode necessary for Sweden's strategy of flexible dispersion of its military aircraft around the country with take-off and landing operations from short, narrow roadstrips. The STOL capability avoids the expense of variable geometry wings which would otherwise be necessary.

An important goal of the Gripen project was to reverse the previous trend toward heavier and more expensive aircraft without sacrificing crucial capabilities. The key was to introduce extensive use of new technology to sharply reduce the weight and size of the aircraft. The latest innovations in engine design permit sufficient thrust from engines weighing half as much, requiring 30% fewer parts and significantly lower fuel consumption than their predecessors. Some 30% of the Gripen's airframe will consist of carbon-fibre-reinforced composites which save 25% in weight for a given strength. Thus, according to plan, the Gripen will weigh about 52% of the Viggen, cost substantially less, and with the aid of fly-by-wire control systems and advanced innovations in computers, radar, and electronic display systems, be capable of equivalent or superior performance.

An industrial consortium, the JAS Industrial Group, was established to build the Gripen. Its members consist of the aircraft division of Saab-Scania at Linköping, Volvo Flygmotor at Trollhattan, Ericsson Radio Systems of Stockholm and Mölndal, and the FFV (Förenade-Fabriksverken—the National Defense Factories Group) Aerotech division at Arboga.

When the Swedish government decided to produce the JAS-39 Gripen, it imposed a list of demands on industry, several of which are of particular interest to the issue of economic conversion. In addition to size, weight, and cost constraints, the government required increased international cooperation with a view to reducing costs, and a reduction of 50% in the number of persons employed in military research and development, and production. A specific requirement was established that the participating organizations make increased efforts to expand their civil activities.

In contrast to the production of about 330 Viggen aircraft, a production run of only about 140 Gripen is contemplated until the end of the century.[31] Saab aircraft division executives estimate the direct production hours required to produce the Gripen at 30,000, compared with 50,000 for the Viggen. Thus, the Gripen order will not fully utilize Saab workshops. In addition, foreign producers will supply about 40% of the Gripen's parts. Figure 5.1 illustrates the major foreign participants and their Swedish industrial links.

The US is represented via General Electric, Hughes Aircraft, Goodyear International, Lear Siegler, Sundstrand, and Teledyne.

It is clear that the Swedish government was a tough bargainer in the decision to proceed with the Gripen project. In addition to procuring an advanced high-capability military aircraft, the government established other goals. It demanded, from the members of the JAS Industrial Group, future expansion in regions suffering from weak employment conditions, the utilization of Swedish subcontractors when they are "competitive," and maximum technology transfer. In addition, General Electric committed itself to co-production of the engine with Volvo Flygmotor, additional procurement and collaboration with Swedish industry in the range of $300–$400 million, a special Science and Technology exhibition in Stockholm jointly sponsored with the JAS Industrial Group to introduce GE to Swedish industry, and a purchasing conference in the US to introduce Swedish industry to GE purchasing officials. In addition, eight technical seminars will be held in various cities throughout Sweden.

The Swedish government also demanded direct offset commitments from large foreign subcontractors for the members of the JAS Industrial Group and other Swedish firms.[32] Many foreign companies are now involved in the Gripen project and the resulting contracts are expected to lead to future orders for Swedish industry. To the extent to which they are for civil products, the government will have succeeded in using a military project to enhance the civil activities of its defense producers.

There appears to be a certain complementarity between military and civil production, at least in the aerospace industry. Thus, a Saab executive noted that his firm probably would not have obtained the Gripen contract without first entering into its commercial aircraft projects. He stressed the technological and economic interactions. Thus, without its civil projects, Saab would not have been able to keep its bid low enough to obtain the military contract. In his view, both military and civil work are necessary to maintain an adequate base.

The Swedish Position on Offsets and Counter-Trade. The Swedish position on offsets and counter-trade is rather complicated. As noted above, in the case of the JAS-39 Gripen aircraft procurement, the government has stressed the importance of maximizing the possibilities for offset business between large foreign subcontractors directly with major Swedish firms comprising the JAS Industrial Group, and indirectly with other Swedish companies. A JAS Industrial Office has been established as the central element in the Industrial Offset Organization with the principal task of advising the US and European governments and industry in identifying appropriate Swedish subcontractor firms. A JAS spokesman estimated that perhaps 5% of Swedish trade now reflected offsets and counter-trade and the figure could reach 8 to 9% by 1990.

Conversely, the Swedish government and Swedish industrialists appear to disapprove of establishing counter-trade requirements as a strict condition for Swedish purchases from abroad. A Saab executive observed that Swedish industry is "kept alive" by free competition on world markets and that it "doesn't believe in offsets." In his opinion, it was more important to be allowed to compete free of protectionism and to develop business relations with the important foreign firms that will be participating in the Gripen project than to force such firms to use Swedish firms as suppliers. Similar views were expressed in a recent government statement. Thus:

> From the standpoint of industrial policy, transactions of the counter-trade type are not the prime goal. It is of greater interest to Swedish industry if the foreign defense industries, which supply goods to Sweden, are engaged or used for the spreading of knowledge to Swedish industry, or make it possible for Swedish industry to get access to and collaborate in foreign and sometimes difficult markets. The purpose of this type of operation—entirely on a commercial basis—is to try to create more long-term, permanent business connections, which in turn are of greater benefit to Swedish industry and society than the traditionally limited counter-trade transactions. (pp. 2–3)

> The question of counter-trade transactions was most recently dealt with in Government Bill 1981/82:102 (p. 127). The view put forward there was that Sweden should not normally make formal demands for counter-trade. In the case of large procurements of defence materiel from abroad, however, it should always be considered if, and how, Swedish industry can be given the opportunity of participating. Various ways of increasing trade, such as industrial cooperation, technology exchange, and the elimination of trade barriers for Swedish exports, should in [the] future be discussed in connection with Swedish defence procurements abroad . . .(p. 3)

> . . . not only the defence industry but also other Swedish industry can be involved in industrial collaboration. Consequently, Swedish industry other than the defence industry can participate in connection with large defence procurements abroad, and this in turn places great demands on coordination and the striking of a balance btween the interests of the defence organization and other national interests such as those of industrial, labour-market, and regional policies. (p. 4)

> The objectives for the projects which come into being through industrial collaboration should in general be to establish long-term co-operation between Swedish and foreign industry. The projects should also create employment in Sweden and/or lead to an influx of valuable know-how to Sweden. In order to ensure that the project lasts for a length of time which exceeds the period required for the procurement of military equipment, it is essential that projects are commercially sound (pp. 4–5).

> "the aim of industrial collaboration should primarily be to:

> a) ensure that the procurements for defence purposes as far as possible give rise to employment opportunities in Sweden within interesting and long-term growth industries;
> b) ensure that the maintenance of the defence materiel purchased can be carried out in Sweden;
> c) stimulate the technological advance of industry by the transfer of technology and know-how to Swedish industry and thereby strengthen . . . the international competitiveness of industry;
> d) promote regional balance in the distribution of job opportunities and industrial activity;

e) improve the ability of Swedish industry to market its goods on international markets and successfully defend the Swedish home market;

f) improve the terms of trade between the countries (p. 5).

Attention should also be paid to the ability of the defence industry to support development in civilian industry within adjacent areas of economic activity" (p. 5).[33]

This rather extensive quotation is included because of its obvious interest for economic conversion. Of course, Sweden's dependence on international trade is well-known. For example, 80% of Saab-Scania's truck output is exported each year. It is nevertheless, most interesting to see the stress placed on the development of civil industry as an important by-product of Swedish procurement of military equipment from abroad.

Summary

It appears that the government program most widely utilized by firms expanding their operations in civil markets is the provision of financial aid by the Industrifonden with provision for repayment on a royalty basis if the product is successful. Both Saab and Volvo Flygmotor have used such funds to finance their collaborative ventures in civil aircraft and civil aeroengines with American partners. Both Swedish firms expect the projects to be highly successful with the government earning an excellent return on its original investment. It was emphasized in each case that substantial amounts of company funds were also at risk in the projects.

Many of the other government aid programs described above either are unknown to defense industry officials or are not viewed as relevant to ease the military to civil resource shift. It was implied by the more important defense producers that easing the current policy of restriction on military exports would be a more important form of aid than most of the other policies available in the government tool kit since in the final analysis, what the firms will need most are alternate markets.

In the case of the JAS-39 Gripen project, the conscious effort to increase the share of foreign participation will limit the military dependence of Swedish firms and the quid-pro-quo of offset requirements, if successful, could expand the markets for Swedish industry.

Notes

1. This section is based, in part, on "Industrial Policy in Sweden," Swedish Ministry of Industry, March 1984, mimeographed.

2. Swedish labor market policies will be discussed in greater detail below.

3. The basic source of information on this organization consists of two undated documents prepared by the Fund: "Industrifonden 1979–1983" and "This is Industrifonden—The Swedish Industrial Development Fund."

4. SUAB is described in Udis, *From Guns to Butter: Technology Organizations and Reduced Military Spending in Western Europe*, pp. 114–117.

5. This section is based, in part, on Yuill and Allen, *European Regional Incentives*, pp. 60–61, 519–543; and on "Swedish Regional Policy," *Fact Sheets on Sweden* (Stockholm: The Swedish Institute, August, 1983).

6. This section is based, in part, upon "Swedish Labor Market Policy." *Fact Sheets on Sweden* (Stockholm: The Swedish Institute, June, 1983).

7. For an interesting recent view see Gösta Rehn, "Swedish Active Labor Market Policy: Retrospect and Prospect," *Industrial Relations*, Vol. 24, No. 1 (Winter 1985), pp. 62–89. Also of interest is Erik Lundberg, "The Rise and Fall of the Swedish Model", *Journal of Economic Literature*, Vol. XXII, No. 1 (March 1985), pp. 1–36.

8. "Swedish Labor Market Policy," p. 1.

9. Sweden's labor market successes have recently been explained in the following terms: "Job creation programmes, retraining schemes and other measures to boost the mobility of workers have helped to keep the Swedish labour market well oiled. Some 4% of the labour force are currently on special job-creation or retraining schemes. Critics who claim that these are not 'proper' jobs, and that true unemployment is more than double the official total, miss the point. By keeping laid-off workers in touch with the job market, Sweden has achieved a better trade-off between unemployment and inflation. . . . An important additional factor is that although unemployment benefits are fairly generous in Sweden, and thus might create a disincentive to work, there are strict controls on eligibility for them. If an unemployed worker refuses to accept a job or training place, his benefit can be stopped. This sanction is only politically acceptable because Sweden can guarantee the unemployed jobs or training places." See *The Economist*, March 7, 1987, pp. 21–26, especially pp. 22–25.

10. The first four titles and descriptions are taken from Inga Thorsson, *et al.*, *In Pursuit of Disarmament: Coversion form Military to Civil Production in Sweden*, Vol. IA (Stockholm: Liber Allmanna Forlaget, 1984), pp. 34–35. The last two titles were provided by Dr. Milton Leitenberg of the Swedish Institute for International Affairs.

11. Thorsson, *et al.*, *In Pursuit of Disarmament*, Vol. 1B, pp. 30–31. The authors note that, "In line with the terms of reference of this study, disarmament scenarios have been elaborated which can reasonably be expected to occur under *favourable conditions*." (Emphasis in original, p. 48.)

12. Thorsson, *et al.*, *In Pursuit of Disarmament*, p. 31.

13. Thorsson, *et al.*, *In Pursuit of Disarmament*, pp. 35–36.

14. Thorsson, *et al.*, *In Pursuit of Disarmament*, p. 36.

15. Thorsson, *et al.*, *In Pursuit of Disarmament*, p. 39.

16. Thorsson, *et al.*, *In Pursuit of Disarmament*, p. 39.

17. Thorsson, *et al.*, *In Pursuit of Disarmament*, p. 47. Further elaboration of the rationale for special consideration of the defense sector appears on pp. 56–57.

18. Thorsson, *et al.*, *In Pursuit of Disarmament*, p. 47.

19. Thorsson, *et al.*, *In Pursuit of Disarmament*, pp. 52–53.

20. Thorsson, *et al.*, *In Pursuit of Disarmament*, p. 54.

21. Thorsson, *et al.*, *In Pursuit of Disarmament*, p. 54.

22. Thorsson, *et al.*, *In Pursuit of Disarmament*, pp. 55–56.

23. Thorsson, *et al.*, *In Pursuit of Disarmament*, p. 57.

24. Thorsson, *et al.*, *In Pursuit of Disarmament*, p. 41.

25. Illustrative of this general viewpoint are the papers presented at the International Conference on Conversion of the Military Industry to Civil Production at Lingatan, Lysekil, Sweden, held during the period February 28 to March 3, 1983. However, a recent story in the Swedish press contains several surprises. Apparently the Swedish government will not present a bill to the Parliament (Riksdag) adopting the Thorsson

report's proposed 5% tax on defense materiel exports and establishment of national and local conversion funds. While no official decision has as yet been announced, the defense and industry ministries are reportedly opposed to the proposal, as well as to setting up a special committee to study the conversion concept. Of interest is the opposition to the tax on defense materiel exports by two major labor organizations: the Swedish Trade Union Confederation (LO) and the Metal Worker's Union (METALL), although they do not oppose the idea of establishing a special study group. See *Svenska Dagbladet*, April 7, 1985. The most recent development has been the creation of a special delegation to continue working on the Thorsson proposals but such work is seen more as background for the upcoming United Nations Conference on Development and Disarmament than as a blueprint for actions likely to be taken in Sweden.

26. In a newspaper story concerning the recent acquisition of Allen-Bradley Co. by Rockwell International, a remarkably similar point about the importance of complementarity of product lines is made by Robert Anderson, Rockwell's chairman. See *Wall Street Journal*, January 22, 1985, p. 38.

27. That this does not inhibit the group to a narrow range of militarily-relevant products, however, is illustrated by the work of the subsidiary Bofors Nobelpharma which develops, manufactures, and markets implant systems which utilize titanium for dental rehabilitation. This unique method of tissue intergration has been quite successful, and in late 1983 a special factory for the production of precision components began to operate in the Bofors Ordnance facilities in Karlskoga. A Bofors executive noted that the production is based on technology acquired from the military field regarding production techniques and quality control. He emphasized that the diversification initiative came from the company, not the government.

28. See "Short Brothers, Saab-Scania Join Boeing 7J7 Program," *Aviation Week and space Technology*, March 31, 1986, pp. 32–33.

29. As noted in Chapter 1, under the pressure of low profitability in its aircraft division, Fairchild is withdrawing from its partnership with Saab on the 340. Saab therefore will assume full responsibility for the aircraft having purchased Fairchild's share.

30. A possible follow on order for 12–15 JA37 Viggen Interceptor aircraft to be built in 1989–1990 is under consideration. This would allow Saab-Scania to maintain operation of its facilities during the period before the Gripen enters production. See "Industry Observer," *Aviation Week and Space Technology*, December 22, 1986, p. 13.

31. Cancellation of the Northrop F-20 and delays on the French Rafale have improved the Gripen's export prospects. A more liberal arms export policy could increase the production run. See "Swedes Preparing to Market Gripen to Neutral Nations," *Aviation Week and Space Technology*, December 15, 1986, p. 20.

32. An offset agreement requires that the seller provide the buyer with an opportunity to produce a portion of the final product up to some stated percentage of the original purchase price. If the buyer lacks the technical capability to produce aircraft components, for example, the agreed upon percentage of purchase price may be provided in the form of some other product which the seller agrees to accept. This process is one variation of a group of policies known collectively, as "countertrade." A member of the JAS management team denies that the Swedish government demanded direct offset commitments and maintains that the offset provision was an outgrowth of competition between such subcontractors as General Electric and Pratt and Whitney. Regardless of their origins, offsets are playing a large role in the Gripen project. Indeed, a recent story attributed delay in choosing air-to-air missiles for the Gripen in part to ". . . a stringent requirement for the government to obtain maximum

offset benefits from any non-Swedish-designed weapon. Up to an additional year may still be required before the final armament decisions are made." See "Swedes Meet Delays in Gripen Development," *Aviation Week and Space Technology*, June 23, 1986, p. 81.

33. All the quoted material is from "Re: Industrial collaboration in procurement of defence materiel from abroad" (Stockholm: Ministry of Defense, Defense Materiel Administration, Transcript. Government Decision, 1983–09–22, signed by Anders Thunborg, Minister of Defense and Christer Dahlberg).

TABLE 5.1 Military Share of Sales and Employment: Major Suppliers to the Swedish Military

Company	1983 Sales (Skr) (in billions)	% of Sales to Military	1983 Employment in Sweden	% of Employment on Military Work
Bofors	4.20	51%	11,000	55%
Ericsson Radio Systems (ERA)	2.20	50	5,800	48
FFV (Forenade Fabriksverken)	3.00	70	8,350	68
Hagglund & Soner	1.30	50	2,550	40
Karlskronavarvet	0.218	60	1,100	91
Kockums	0.200	8	3,400	6
Philips Elektronikindustrier (PEAB)	1.30	50	1,900	60
Saab-Scania Group	20.80	8	32,000	14
Saab Aircraft Division	1.50	91	4,600	81
Saab Combitech	0.694	54	1,700	47
Volvo Group	100.00	.6	76,000	2
Volvo Flygmotor	1.10	55	2,850	53

Source: Inga Thorsson, et al., Vol. A, pp. 115-125; and interview materials. Some data inconsistencies exist between the two sources but the table is probably useful to indicate general orders of magnitude.

Figure 5.1 Imports of Sub-Systems: JAS Project

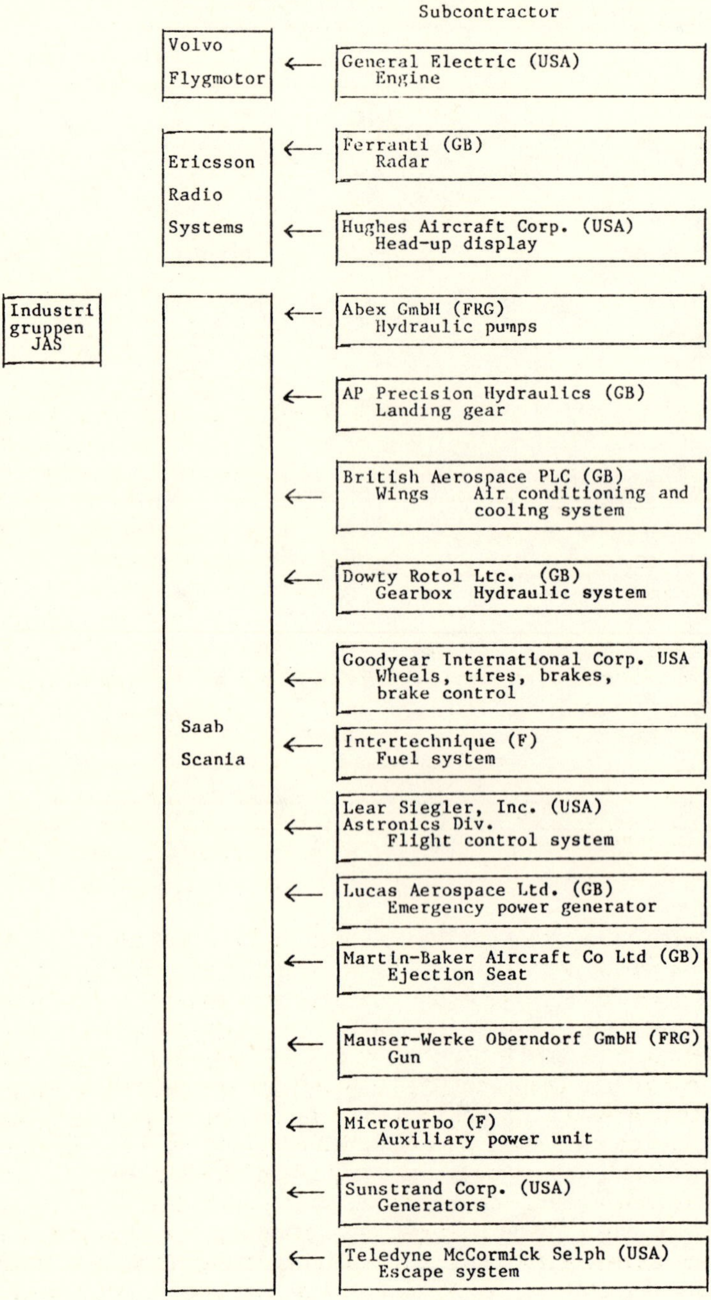

Subcontractor

| Volvo Flygmotor | ← | General Electric (USA) Engine |

| Ericsson Radio Systems | ← | Ferranti (GB) Radar |
| | ← | Hughes Aircraft Corp. (USA) Head-up display |

Industri gruppen JAS

Saab Scania	←	Abex GmbH (FRG) Hydraulic pumps
	←	AP Precision Hydraulics (GB) Landing gear
	←	British Aerospace PLC (GB) Wings Air conditioning and cooling system
	←	Dowty Rotol Ltc. (GB) Gearbox Hydraulic system
	←	Goodyear International Corp. USA Wheels, tires, brakes, brake control
	←	Intertechnique (F) Fuel system
	←	Lear Siegler, Inc. (USA) Astronics Div. Flight control system
	←	Lucas Aerospace Ltd. (GB) Emergency power generator
	←	Martin-Baker Aircraft Co Ltd (GB) Ejection Seat
	←	Mauser-Werke Oberndorf GmbH (FRG) Gun
	←	Microturbo (F) Auxiliary power unit
	←	Sunstrand Corp. (USA) Generators
	←	Teledyne McCormick Selph (USA) Escape system

Source: Inga Thorsson, *et al.*, Vol. 1B, p. 20.

6

United Kingdom

Background on British Industrial Policy[1]

When the British government began to establish a planning machinery in the 1960s, it grew out of concern over the low growth rate of the economy. The attempt resembled the French model in its reliance upon interest group negotiation and consultation. It was designed by an unlikely combination of Labour Party intellectuals and merchant bankers against oppostion from the Conservative party, some business groups, and trade unionists. Thus, no consensus existed, nor was there a bureaucracy which even vaguely resembled that of France where civil servants often had technical and/or business knowledge. The Conservative government of the early 1960s established the National Economic Development Council (NEDC) and a series of Economic Development Councils (EDC's) for particular industries. They were designed to provide forums for discussions of future developments in the national economy and in particular industries. However, there was no coherent plan within which to establish sectoral goals and regional development and section councils often became little more than casual discussion groups. Increased financial help was provided to specific industries prominent among which were aircraft, cotton, ocean shipping, and ship-building.

When the Labour government took office in 1964 it developed a national plan but it failed for a number of reasons which ranged from poor forecasts and the devaluation of the pound to interagency squabbling. In 1967, two important acts were passed: (1) the Industrial Expansion Bill which enabled the government to provide financial aid to specific industries without specific Parliamentary approval, and (2) the Industrial Reorganization Act which set up the Industrial Reorganization Corporation (IRC) to promote efficiency, largely through mergers of firms. The IRC also functioned as a government investment bank by providing equity capital and credit to potential growth companies and funding regional development authorities.

However, when the next Conservative government took power in 1970, promising to reduce government intervention in the economy it abolished the IRC and shrunk the NEDC. The government was forced to reverse its anti-interventionist policy by high unemployment and moved to rescue the ailing Rolls-Royce and Upper Clyde shipbuilders and to pass the Industry Act of 1972 which provided financial help to industry. Section 7 dealt with growth and low interest loans to firms in particular regions. Aid under Section 8 provided grants for general investment and other forms of aid to specific industries. Sixteen industries received Section 8 help between 1972 and September 1978 but the wide variety of industries does not suggest a sharply focused program. The range included textiles, clothing, and red meat slaughterhouses at one end and electronic components, instrumentation and automation, and microelectronics at the other.

The next Labour government which took office in 1974 pushed greater government owership of industry and planning under the NEDC. The National Enterprise Board was set up in 1975 to function as a holding company for most of its equity holdings in private firms. Shipbuilding and aircraft were nationalized in 1977 and Sector Working Parties (SWPs) were established for 37 industries under NEDC. The SWPs were concentrated in manufacturing industries and they were composed of government officials, industrial executives and trade union representatives. While the SWPs generated many policy recommendations they failed to cooperate with the National Enterprise Board and many private firms simply ignored their recommendations.[2] In the late 1970s, the Labour government reduced aid to high-technology industries via both grants for research and development, and aid from the NEB.

The Conservatives returned to power in 1979 under Prime Minister Margaret Thatcher and undertook to sell off much of the government's holdings in nationalized firms. The government also changed the role of the NEDC. The Sector Working Parties either ceased operations or became EDC's to improve communication between government, labor, and industry.

Under the Thatcher government, the composition of aid changed as well with relatively less for sectoral development; research, development, and innovation;[3] and regional assistance; and relatively more for employment and training; and export assistance.

Public Procurement

Such high-technology industries as computers and aircraft have been the principal beneficiaries of preferences in public purchases. The relatively large size of the public sector in the UK makes public procurement a powerful instrument of favoritism. However, public procurement preferences have been declining recently. At the beginning of 1981, the UK began to follow the rules of the General Agreement on Tariffs and Trade (GATT) on Government procurement which do somewhat inhibit such preferences. Poor experiences with such preferences, particularly in civil aircraft, have also contributed to the loss of appeal, although firms located in depressed regions in product areas not covered by the GATT rules still receive such preferential treatment. Also, in late 1980 the government allocated 10 million pounds to help public units utilize their purchases to aid the development of British industry, presumably within the GATT rules. The Offshore Supplies Office of the Energy Department also functions to see to it that British firms receive a "full and fair" opportunity to provide equipment used in offshore oil drilling in British waters.

Tax and Financial Assistance Measures

While most UK tax policy is not industry-specific, there are a few provisions of the tax code which are relevant to this inquiry. One set of such rules encourages R&D. All assets used for R&D may be fully depreciated in one year. This is more liberal than the general rule as regards the depreciation of buildings. Also, firms may treat all payments to research associations as current expenses. Industry-specific tax rules apply in shipbuilding. Shipbuilders receive tax forgiveness in an amount equal to 2% of the contract price of their ships while commercial vessels which weigh more than 15 tons are exempt from the value-added tax (normally 15% on domestic sales and zero on exports).

Financial aid is granted via loan guarantees, low interest loans, cover for exchange rate variation, and equity itself. In recent years stress has shifted from assisting older basic industries to high-technology firms. Equity investments are available for nationalized firms in depressed sectors and special programs exist to assist the shipbuilding and aircraft industries. So-called launch aid has been available since 1949 under which the government may fund 50% of market development costs of new aircraft or aeroengines. While the agreements require repayment, the government has always lost money on such aid.[4] The principal rationale for such aid has been the presumed unavailability of adequate capital at fixed and reasonable interest rates in European capital markets.

Financial help to the shipbuilding industry takes two forms: an intervention fund and the home credit plan. The first dates to 1977 and is designed to assist UK shipyards to compete in the international market. The size of the fund and the maximum allowable aid per order have both been reduced since 1979. The home credit plan makes available to British buyers terms comparable to those offered by the credit agencies of other countries to buyers of their vessels and to those made available to foreign buyers of British ships via the British Export Credit Guarantee Department (ECGD).

The Industrial Development Act of 1982 authorizes via its Section 8, various forms of financial aid to industry. Such aid funds capital projects which would otherwise probably not be located in the UK. Thus, large, multinational firms are the principal beneficiaries. Since Section 8 aid is not available for projects below a certain minimum size, a loan guarantee program available only to small firms was also initiated. Section 8 aid is available to all projects viewed as in the national interest and commercially promising, provided the project also could easily be located abroad and would significantly benefit the performance of the industry. Finally the project must be likely to increase UK output or bring a major innovation to the country. Under these general criteria, the mechanical and electrical engineering industries led with 25.4% and 18.9% of this aid, respectively. The average aid equaled 11.6% of the costs of all assisted projects.

Section 8 also has three major non-sectorally specific programs: a loan guarantee program for smaller firms, an energy conservation program, and a selective investment program. None appear to bear specifically on the military to civil shift of resources.

Twenty-four sector-specific plans have been funded under Section 8. Prior to the Conservative Party victory in 1979 such programs were focused on mature industries. Since 1979 the focus has shifted to new high-technology areas. Several of these schemes may be relevant to our interests. The private sector steel plan involves three forms of help. Payments made to discharged workers can be covered up to 85%. Grants equal to 25% of the cost of closing or restructuring plants are available. The steel industry also has agreed to build up a fund to pay facilities closing costs of its members. Grants up to 25% of the total amount of this fund are available. It is estimated that discharged employees will receive about 36% of the aid under the program, 21% will go to firms for meeting closing or restructuring costs, and 43% will go to the industry's fund. Under the steel castings arrangement, grants are available for a fund that reimburses firms engaged in facilities shutdown. Further, favorable tax treatment applies to industry payments to such funds.

Grants for consulting studies and installation costs of flexible manufacturing systems are available under the Flexible Manufacturing Systems Scheme (FMSS). If a consultant who has been approved by the Department of Trade and Industry (DTI) is utilized, the government will pay half of consulting fees up to a maximum of 50,000 pounds. One third of installation costs may also be reimbursed. Under the similar Robot Support Program, one third of the cost of installing robots may be covered plus 50% of the cost of studies by approved consultants. The cost of consultants falls under the Support for Innovation program to be discussed below. Part of the costs of designing, developing, and launching new products or processes in fibre optics may be funded jointly under Section 8 and the Support for Innovation program. Grants in an amount up to 60,000 pounds are available to pay one third of the costs of acquiring and installing computer-aided design and test equipment.

The costs of capital equipment purchases by small engineering firms employing less than 200 persons are aided by the Small Engineering Firms Investment Scheme (SEFIS). One third of the eligible costs of a project may be covered up to a maxium of 200,000 pounds, excluding value-added tax, regional development grants, and European Community grants. The program was very popular and was modified in March 1983 to apply to firms employing up to 500 persons and not restricted to the engineering industries.

With few exceptions, the Section 8 assistance programs begun under the current Conservative government are not industry-specific and have supported the purchase of equipment in a wide variety of industries. While keyed to the acquistion of particular types of equipment (like computer-aided design), such equipment need not be produced in the UK. Some industry quarters, therefore, feel that the combined impact of these programs is more likely to aid British firms using the equipment, rather than those producing it.

Exchange Rate Insurance. British borrowers of foreign currency from European Community lending institutions may be insured against losses resulting from exchange rate variations under a 1978 amendment to Section 8. Cost of such loans including the exchange rate cover is about 3% lower than those denominated in British pounds.

Export Credits. The Export Credit Guarantee Department (ECGD) provides loan guarantees and low interest loans to finance British exports. The shipbuilding and aircraft industries appear to receive better terms under this aid program than those available to other sectors of British industry. It has been estimated that ECGD loan guarantees cover a third of UK exports while direct loans under the program are involved in supporting 5% of British exports.[5] Various OECD arrangements set minimum terms for export credit financing but ships and aircraft are highly competitive products and thus the terms permitted for them are generally more liberal than for other exported products.

Financial Aid to Innovation: The British Technology Group

The British Technology Group was established in 1981 as an umbrella organization to link two older organizations whose missions had become quite similar: the National Research Development Corporation (NRDC) and the National Enterprise Board (NEB). Both organizations were supplying equity capital to innovative firms. The NRDC was set up in 1949 to encourage the exploitation by private firms of public sector research results. It also attempted to license publicly held patents and until mid-1983 held rights of first refusal on the patents of public research laboratories and universities. The NRDC acquires patents from private inventors on occasion as well. Table 6.1 shows the number of inventions submitted to NRDC by source and indicates the major role of the universities. In the view of government officials, the qualitatively most important originate in the public sector.

The NRDC will enter into joint ventures with private organizations and its investments in such projects were in the vicinity of 12 million pounds annually in the fiscal years 1980–1982.

The early rationale for NRDC was that there were many interesting ideas "lying around" in government laboratories but the research scientists were unlikely to know how to exploit them, even if they could raise funds. It should be emphasized that the NRDC was never a rescue operation to save "lame ducks." In exploiting inventions, it operated along lines similar to ANVAR in France.

The NEB began operations in 1975. Until 1979 its activities were largely devoted to aiding four troubled firms: British Leyland, Rolls-Royce, Alfred Herbert, and Cambridge Instruments. Almost 90% of its funds spent to March 1979 went to those four companies. While originally formed to advance the public ownership of British industry, its mission was altered by the new Conservative government. Currently it is to encourage the ownership of industry by private capital and it now sells its shares of private firms when they become profitable. Its borrowing authority has been reduced and under the privatization policy of the Conservative government it has had to sell a number of its shareholdings, most recently in British Telecommunications.

NEB's focus has also drifted from troubled firms to the high-technology sector. British Leyland and Rolls-Royce have been transferred to the Department of Trade and Industry. Cambridge Instruments has been sold as were the remaining assets of the collapsed Alfred Herbert. Of its industrial investments of 141.6 million pounds at the end of calendar 1982, about two thirds, or $228 million, was in five firms: Inmos, an integrated circuit manufacturer; Data Recording Instrument Company, Ltd., a maker of computer peripherals; Wholesale Vehicle Finance, Ltd., which finance British Leyland distributors; British Underwater Engineering, a supplier of underwater services, vessels, design engineering, and products manufactured for the offshore oil industry; and Monotype Holdings, a producer of typesetting equipment (including computerized laser-based systems).

Under both political parties the NEB has failed to reach the financial goals established for it by the government and it has earned a substantially lower rate of return on investment than that realized by private investors.

An official of the British Technology Group commented that NEB would shortly cease to have a role to play (as privatization is completed) and would "quietly go out of business." This process has taken somewhat longer than anticipated, however, and by the summer of 1986 the NEB was still in existence. As a result of its divestment program its total holdings had been reduced to just six investments with these to be disposed of as soon as practicable. Over the past two years or so its divestment program has raised 200 million pounds of Public Dividend Capital which BTG has repaid to the Exchequer.

In November 1984, BTG announced a new corporate plan for itself under which it will concentrate its efforts on technology transfer, aiding British industry to exploit technology from UK public sector sources.[6]

Specifically, BTG will:

- offer to take responsibility for patenting, or otherwise protecting, technology derived from universities and other public sector sources;
- provide funding for the development of that technology to the point where it can be taken up by industry;
- transfer the technology to industry by seeking licensees;
- offer project finance to help those licensees to launch the product onto the market;
- share the license income with the source of the technology, either the institution or the inventor; and
- plough back its retained share of the license income into the development and exploitation of other technology.

As part of its technology transfer role, BTG will also offer project finance to companies that want to develop new products and processes, based on their own new technology. In cases where a particular technology requires the setting-up of a new company, BTG will perform a catalytic role in promoting the creation of start-up companies. All these activities will be carried out on commercial terms. BTG expects to be both profit-making and self-financing throughout the period of the 1984–1989 five-year plan.

BTG also announced the following initiatives to forward its technology transfer goals:

- BTG will invest about 15 million pounds per year from its own resources, doubling its current rate of investment in development projects at universities and other public sector sources.
- BTG will provide finance for methods of technology transfer in addition to its traditional support of inventions through licensing.

It will offer up to 50% of the finance required for projects to support contract R&D, consultancy work, and other services provided by university departments and industrial liaison companies. This finance will be offered on commercial terms and BTG will expect to recover its investment from the revenues generated by these institutions.

A new initiative called "Campus Investments" will specialize in providing finance for academic spin-off and start-up companies.[7]

- In the fall of 1985 BTG announced the winner of the Third Academic Enterprise Competition for academic researchers involved in setting up a new company to exploit their research results; the 25,000 pound award went to an Oxford University researcher for his work on a robotvision system. A 10,000 pound second prize was also awarded. No competition was held in 1986 and at this writing no decision has been made on the continuance of the program. BTG is compiling a new computer database to assist inventors and potential licensees in the preliminary matching of new ideas with possible industrial users.
- BTG will begin to share royalty income with all sources of inventions. It will also increase the share of royalty income paid to the source during the early stages of the exploitation of an invention.
- Forty-two universities have agreed that in the future the leaders of BTG funded projects will be designated BTG Research Fellows.
- BTG has set up an eight-man liaison team (4 full-time, 4 part-time) whose role will be to seek out commercial opportunities by visiting laboratories throughout the UK. Regular portfolio reviews will also be introduced to improve communications and keep institutions better informed of progress in exploiting their inventions.

Nationalized Industries

Historically, the nationalization process has been used to channel government funds to depressed industries not otherwise likely to have been able to attract private capital. Often the nationalized firms had difficulty in attaining profitability because they were used to forward other government goals such as expanding in depressed regions or otherwise maintaining employment.[8] Beyond the BTG's holdings, the government owns large parts of other industries. These include the airline, steel, coal, automobile, and shipbuilding industries. The Thatcher government is in the process of reducing its ownership of industry and in a well-publicized venture, recently sold British Telecommunications to private investors at very successful terms for the government. However, the government will often sell only a portion of the shares of the firms it owns under an arrangement where it promises not to involve itself with the management provided the government's investment is safe and earning a competitive return.

Science and Technology

The British government financially supports R&D and attempts to make technology more widely available to firms. Support to industry-based science and technology activities tend not to be industry-specific, with the outstanding exceptions of R&D support for the aerospace and electronics industries. In 1981 government aid financed 68% of aerospace industry R&D, 50% of electronics industry R&D, and only 34% of all manufacturing R&D. Individual firms retain the rights to any patents resulting from their involvement in government-supported research, but if the patent remains unexploited after three years, the government has the right to use such results.

Programs of the Department of Trade and Industry. The DTI is the principal instrument for government support for industrial R&D but it accounts for a relatively small share of the government's aggregate research budget— 8.6% in 1984–1985. The DTI proportion of government *civil* department expenditure was 18% in the same period. The latest Science and Technology report indicates a total departmental expenditure of 376 million pounds. Industry received 63% of this funding, space 17%, aviation 8.5% and DTI's own four research laboratories, 10%. Until recently DTI had six research laboratories but two of them, the National Maritime Institute and the Computer Aided Design Center, were transferred to private status in 1982 and 1983, respectively. The remaining laboratories do work for other government agencies and for industry, as well as for DTI.

The main program for funding industrial R&D is the DTI's Support for Innovation Scheme (SFI).[9] It is designed to encourage innovative products or processes which promise high returns. For single companies grants of up to 25% of project costs are available; for collaborative ventures involving at least 3 partners grants of up to 50% may be available. To qualify for assistance firms must demonstrate that:

1. Projects are innovative and represent a significant advance for the industry concerned;
2. government assistance is necessary to meet these aims;
3. they operate in the UK.

Other forms of support offered by DTI include Business and Technical Advisory Services, national and regional investment programmes and exports. Aid under the SFI program falls into five areas: R&D projects leading to new products and process developments, longer term applied R&D, market studies, production launch, and preproduction orders. Although the last area has been suspended it represents a rather interesting approach. Under it, DTI would buy a new product and allow prospective purchasers to use it for a trial period. If the user was satisfied, DTI expected him to buy the product after the trial period.

A major purpose of most of these programs is enhanced awareness of the technologies used and there are special SFI schemes to aid in the dissemination of this knowledge. Free consulting is provided by the Manufacturing Advisory Service, the Design Advisory Service, the Small firms Technical Enquiry Service, and the Quality Assurance Advisory Service. Exhibitions, conferences, seminars and courses are also provided.

One program in particular is worth attention. It is known as the Alvey program and focuses on collaborative research dealing with information technology; very large scale intergration (VLSI); software; man-machine interfaces; and intelligent knowledge-based systems.[10] Each project involves at least two research institutions. The government was prepared to pay 50 million pounds in support of an academic research undertaking and 150 million pounds in aid of the industry research effort. These funds were to come from DTI, the Department of Education and Science, and the Ministry of Defense and be spent over a term of five years. The relatively large support package for industry research has been rationalized by the fact that Alvey program research is further removed from commercial application than is most SFI funded projects.

In November 1984, the Minister of State for Industry and Information Technology announced that the Department would accept no new applications under the Support for Innovation program pending the completion of a five-month review of the Department's programs of support for industrial research and development.

The Secretary of State for Trade and Industry announced the results of the review in late March 1985. The Government concluded that more money would be made available for collaborative research, advisory services, and schemes for encouraging "best practices" and improving key skills. However, support for projects in individual firms would be reduced. The goal is to concentrate support on innovative projects representing significant advances for the industry or sector involved. Microelectronics, fibre-optics, and computer software continue to be viewed as key technologies for support. While aid to aircraft and aircraft engine R&D will continue, it will be at reduced levels.

Aid to Aerospace. The British government has used nationalization of firms as a device to speed rationalization in the industry. Short Brothers, producers of commuter and small transport aircraft is now wholly-owned by the government. In 1977, British Aerospace (BA) was formed by merging several independent companies, principally Hawker-Sideley and British Aircraft Corporation. The firm is now 48.43% owned by the government, 48.43% by private shareholders, and 3.14% employee owned. Prior to 1982 BA was 100% state-owned.

Launch aid is also provided by the government and consists of up to 50% of development cost of aircraft projects which seemingly cannot be funded privately. It apparently provided a model for the recently adopted Swedish Industrifonden. Launch aid has also been provided for the W30 helicopter and the RB-211 Rolls-Royce engine for the Boeing 757 aircraft.

The UK and Italy agreed in 1984 to produce the EH-101 helicopter for both military and civil use. Westland of the UK and Construzioni Aeronautiche Giovanni Augusta S.p.A. of Italy are the principal partner firms, with both nations providing launch aid. Despite some uncertainties when Westland encountered severe financial problems in 1985, the program appears to be running smoothly. Deliveries to the navies of the partner states are planned for 1990, with civil certification anticipated in 1989.[11] Direct funding is also provided for aircraft and engine projects for Airbus Industrie. However, despite general optimism among Airbus Industrie officials that recent successes will pave the way for easier financing for larger models (the A330 and A340), funding appears to be least certain in the UK, where the government has indicated reluctance to finance another Airbus project.[12] Most recently there have been suggestions that all may not be well in the financial position of the German Airbus partner.[13]

Regional Policy[14]

British regional policy has recently undergone substantial changes after a review in a White Paper on Regional Industrial Development.[15] The review took a skeptical position on the need for regional policy and raised the issues of the cost-effectiveness of regional aid measures; a bias towards capital-intensive and manufacturing industry projects; and the possibility that the British economy may have been damaged by unsound location policies. The resulting proposals place greater stress on job creation, more selectivity, less automatic assistance and less discrimination against service activities.

Regional Development Grants (RDG) will be retained but with a reduced role. They will be project-related rather than asset-related, and will be available only for projects which create new capacity, extend existing capacity, or bring a change in product, process, or service. These changes will bring the program in line with European Commission standards and thereby, bring in EEC funds to help meet program costs. In addition, there will be a 10,000 pound cost per job ceiling except for small firm's with fewer than 200 workers and projects with eligible expenditure of 500,000 pounds or less. Certain service industries will now be qualified for aid. Planned RDG expenditures will probably decline as a result of these changes.

Regional selective assistance is discretionary project-related assistance which normally takes the form of capital grants, training grants or exchange risk cover for European loans. While other forms of assistance (particularly soft loans, but also equity finance and loan guarantees) have been used on occasions in the past, such assistance is now rare.

Two alternative aid packages exist for Northern Ireland. Under the first, a standard and generally automatic capital grant of 20% of eligible expenditures exists. The second is a much more discretionary bundle of selective aid including industrial development grants of up to 50% of eligible expenditure, employment grants, interest relief grants and soft loans, and a corporate tax relief grant. This last feature is new and it provides a reimbursement of up to 80% of the corporate tax paid by firms on profits from projects for which an application for selective assistance has been made. In effect the recipient of such a grant could pay as little as 10.4% of eligible profits compared with the UK average rate of 52%.[16] In addition, other provisions extend the incentives to existing firms as well as new firms, and provide a management incentives plan which helps firms recruit managers to Northern Ireland at or above market salaries. Northern Ireland also qualifies for such standard British incentives as the ability to use government factories at low rents and various worker mobility schemes.

Over time there has been a substantial cutback in the coverage of assisted areas. For example, in 1979, 44% of the working population was located in such areas. By 1982 the figure had been reduced to 27%. As a result of heavy cutbacks in car manufacturing and the metal industry, the West Midlands area (near Birmingham) was designated for assistance in late 1984. This increased the share of the working population covered up to 35%, but only 15% are covered by the full battery of aid devices.

There is substantial geographic concentration expecially among the older basic industries like steel and coal. Thus, policies to alleviate depressed regions often overlap with those aimed at employee redundancy. While the UK operates programs of income maintenance, aid to worker mobility, and worker retraining, it is important to note that several are industry-specific, and within these, some are designed to meet European Community standards. The Steel Redundancy Program is an example of a program which meets EEC standards and thus qualifies for EEC financial aid. It should be noted that this scheme is much more generous than any other purely UK program, providing, as it does, continuing income support and retraining. There are also special UK programs for the coal and shipbuilding industries which, in turn, are more generous than non-industry-specific UK programs. A government official expressed the goals of these programs as "getting the works closed without riots in the streets."

Also of interest are several efforts which strive to help redundant workers to form small businesses. British Steel Corporation in particular has provided advice on this subject to its workers made redundant by works closures. The Coal Board has also engaged in similar activities. Pilkington Glass went a step further and established a trust activity with the purpose of giving advice on investment, skill use, etc., and the company also put some of its premises at the disposal of the trust. These innovative efforts are worthy of further investigation.

Dependence on the Military Customer and the Government

There are several factors which suggest that defense producers in the UK may be facing some market problems in the foreseeable future. While no one in authority speaks of substantial reductions in British military spending, these factors should be recognized. The first is the government's position that it is coming to the end of its commitment to expand defense spending by 3% per year in real terms. The second factor is the possible collision course between a relatively level course of aggregate defense spending and growing expenditures on the British Trident submarine program, the heart of the UK deterrent force. There is substantial concern in some quarters concerning the inevitable squeeze on conventional forces, whose value is widely believed to have been demonstrated during the Falklands War. The dilemma, if anything, is deepened by speculation concerning the impact of the new US Strategic Defense Initative on the role of the British and French deterrent forces.

A Ministry of Defense official speculated on what role the government would take if major defense producers found themselves in substantial distress. He noted that it would be imperative, politically to do something but added, "this government is less inclined than most to go very far in that direction; we don't feel that it is our responsibility to prime the pump." On the other hand, the present government sees itself as a large, prudent buyer in the defense market and would like to use its purchasing power to make sure that the firms are competitive. In an effort eventually to privatize the Royal Arsenals the government has "pushed R&D capability and marketing skills into them and now contracts with them on a commercial basis."

While there is nothing in the UK comparable to the US Defense Department's Office of Economic Adjustment, the British MOD has engaged in discussions with other departments designed to encourage industry and local governments to bring other industry into areas being vacated by the military. There are apparently non-governmental Local Authority Conversion Councils which consider alternative ways to utilize such facilities. However, there is no MOD intention to "pour lots of money into such efforts."

My respondent noted that "while the MOD would like to help British suppliers become 'lean and fit,' in the final analysis the MOD is a customer and not a client. Therefore, we would not hesitate to look for a more efficient European industrial base, if it were necessary to rationalize the industry." Others, however, would be skeptical of allowing crucial defense production facilities to go "offshore," given the diverse political reaction abroad to Britain's Falklands War.

On the other hand, the British government risked the ire of British workers, unions, and members of Parliament from both Conservative and Labour parties in late 1986 when it selected the Boeing E-3 airborne warning and control system (AWACS) in preference to the British General Electric Company (GEC) Avionics Nimrod AEW Mk.3 airborne early warning program. The decision came after the equivalent of $1.3 billion had been spent by the British over a nine year period in an attempt to bring the Nimrod to an acceptable level of performance. While the decision is clearly a blow to the prestige of British GEC, its impact on other firms and on employment is more difficult to predict since Boeing has agreed to put offset work equal to 130% of the value of the more expensive AWACS contract into the UK. This case indicates that when necessary military equipment available from a foreign source is clearly superior to British models, the government will go offshore. In this instance the British government team appears to have come out with a good bargain in terms of the offset conditions.[17]

Major British firms engaged in defense production are attempting to broaden their civil and export markets, although in some cases, the degree of defense dependency is suprisingly low. Thus, while British Aerospace's largest single customer is the British government, such sales constitute only about a fourth of total sales, and of this amount, three-fourths are for the military. This puts BA's domestic military sales at just under 19% of the total. Of course, since some 60% of total sales are exported, and military sales are included in that figure, the company's total dependence on military customers in all its markets certainly exceeds the 19% figure. Unfortunately, at this writing, the figures are lacking, and an exact amount can not be determined. It is worth noting, however, how deeply BA is engaged in joint products on both the civil and military markets. It is a partner in Airbus with the French, Germans, and Spanish; on the Concorde and Jaguar with French firms; on the Hawk trainer and several generations of Harriers with McDonnell-Douglas of the US; and on the Tornado with West Germany and Italy. If the European Fighter Aircraft actually is built, BA will work with West German, Spanish, and Italian partners. The BAe 146 civil airliner which is viewed as British is done with Avco Lycoming engines (US) and with Saab participating in the production of the wings. Apparently the company was surprised by the success of its BAe 146 in the United States as it was designed originally as a workhorse for third world markets. British Aerospace executives now maintain that the days of producing principally for the British market are over, and that, to be successful, products must be suitable for other markets as well. The company believes that there are "tremendous possibilities" in civil aircraft and is confident that it can "get its share."

The story is similar at Rolls-Royce with major emphasis on exports and collaboration. Rolls-Royce executives estimate the cost of developing a new engine from scratch at $1.5 billion and conclude that there are few firms able to afford such a cost on their own.[18] The company is currently engaged in collaboration with Pratt and Whitney of the US and with Japanese producers on an engine to power an aircraft with a capacity of 150 seats. They also are working with GE on engines to power medium and long-range aircraft. Volvo Flygmotor is producing engines under license with Rolls-Royce, and MTU of West Germany and Fiat of Italy are partners with

Rolls-Royce on the RB 199 engine which powers the Tornado. Rolls-Royce and Turbomeca of France provide the Adour engine for the Jaguar and Hawk military aircraft. Less well-known is Rolls-Royce's role in providing the nuclear plant for the British Trident submarine program.

Rolls-Royce sales are divided almost evenly between the United Kingdom and exports, with most domestic sales going to the government. The company believes that there is overcapacity in aeroengine capacity in world markets today, and that there is one extra producer—"but it isn't Rolls-Royce."

Spin-off and Diversification

Over the years, and regardless of the political party in power, the UK has consistently tried to speed up the transfer of technology between sectors of the British economy; from the early beginnings in the post-WWII period by the NRDC to find uses for the many patents developed in government laboratories and with government aid to the more modern programs described above.

In his foreward to the 1984 Science and Technology Report of the Department of Trade and Industry, Geoffrey Pattie, Minister of State for Industry and Technology wrote:

> The Government's first role is to encourage the right market conditions for innovators to thrive in. This means ensuring that the rewards for enterprise act as a strong and proper incentive to research in new ideas, to the design and development of new technologies, and to their commercial application. Through its support for science and technology, the Department can help reinforce this drive to innovate—by bringing together firms and other researchers in collaborative pre-competitive ventures; by providing information and raising awareness of key technologies; and by supporting particularly promising process or product innovation which would not otherwise be successfully developed or exploited in the market place.

In the economist's terms, the government believes that there are external benefits present in supporting these activities.

The array of such programs is impressive. The largest single effort to get spinoff into the country occurs between the DTI and the MOD. The Department of Trade and Industry has placed about 35 million pounds per year into Defense Ministry Laboratories in search of spinoff results. About 24 million of that amount is spent intramurally in MOD laboratories while the balance goes to extramural efforts in firms like Rolls-Royce. The underlying belief is that a large proportion of the technology utilized for defense purposes is applicable to civil uses as well, but that without explicit efforts to publicize them, they would never find their way into civil use.

Yet, the suspicion persists that optimistic expectations have not fully been realized. The reasons for the disappointing results range from indictments of the British caste system which has historically viewed science as an acceptable pursuit for a gentleman but not applied engineering or business, the small home market, inadequate government financial support, and defects of the technology transfer mechanism. The cumulative effect of these problems is seen by some observers as quite serious since it may lead to a brain drain of British scientists to the United States and elsewhere.[19] In mid-1982, a most interesting study of the commercial exploitation of defense techonolgy in the electronics industry was completed by Sir Ieuan Maddock, a distinguished British scientist and retired civil servant. Among its more challenging conclusions was the observation that ". . . technology-push does not work unless it is linked with a great measure of market pull."[20] Sir Ieuan then went on to suggest how this might be attained. Among his other recommendations are a greater degree of centralized purchasing, high-volume ordering and product preference as well as major efforts to influence the MOD to buy standard commercially available products wherever possible rather than very specialized items "tuned to their own needs."[21]

Also of interest are two very recent developments: The establishment of DTE (Defence Technology Enterprises), a company set up by MOD and a City (Financial) company to exploit for civil markets R&D carried by MOD research establishments; and the recently announced national electronic research initiatives (NERI's) whose objective is to secure civil spinoff from defence research in the electronics and information technology fields.

A rather different approach to technology transfer and diversification among defense producers is that attempted by a group of shop stewards at Lucas Aerospace. The attempt has received a great deal of notoriety and "The Lucas Plan" has now become synonymous with grass roots efforts by workers and their supporters to, as it were, invent plow shares to replace swords. While it has begun to assume the qualities of a "movement,"[22] the reality appears far removed from the image. The Corporate Plan is presented in a document prepared by the Lucas Aerospace Combine Shop Steward Committee in the mid-1970s. It is a curious mixture of criticisms of capitalism and proposals for civil production in six major areas, outside of aerospace. The plan reflects a joint desire to prevent unemployment as defense orders decline and to produce "socially-useful" products. According to a Lucas Aerospace executive, two efforts were attempted. One which focused on the production of electric kettles for the consumer market, was a substantial failure. In the second, Lucas management in an old factory complex facing closure in Bradford asked the union to recommend product ideas within the aerospace line. Apparently, the resulting suggestions were quite helpful in the development of samarium cobalt engines which, paradoxically, are utilized in missile production. Not surprisingly, the different parties have widely differing explanations for the relative lack of success of the plan. Two principal issues are raised by the Lucas experience: the role of workers and their representatives in cooperating with management on new product development, and how far afield firms may expect to go to find new products which they are likely to be able to produce and market effectively. It may well be that research into the economics of diversification would throw much useful light onto an area which seems to have received more than its share of heat.[23]

Summary

In a sense, the United Kingdom is in a unique position among the countries studied in Western Europe. It came out of WWII in a much weakened economic position but still a major military and economic power which had emerged victorious from the war and had never been occupied by enemy forces. Dating probably from the withdrawals from "East of Suez" in the mid-1950s the country has been undergoing a painful shrinking process. This is expecially true in the area of military industry in which Britain once held a towering position with capabilities across almost the full range of weaponry, both conventional and nuclear. Thus, it has almost continually been experiencing the transfer of resources from the military to civil sectors or, at least, intramilitary transfers. The continuing market shrinkage has resulted in a rash of corporate mergers. However, each round of mergers of defense firms has been accompanied by a much less than proportionate reduction in defense production capacity. Thus, Britain has been left with such anomalies as the world's largest maker of aeroengines, Rolls-Royce, which can only survive by dependence upon foreign markets. Britain's aircraft and avionics industries are also among the most advanced, but its modest domestic market has made exports and collaborative ventures a way of life in both military and civil markets.

Its partnerships have gone in both directions: trans-Atlantic with the United States on the Harrier and the Hawk, and cross-channel with the French on the Jaguar, several helicopter models and the Concorde; with the French, Germans, and Spanish in the airbus; and with West Germany and Italy on the Tornado. One consequence of these developments is an inevitable reduction in the variety of products being produced which should lead to a greater degree of standardized weapons in NATO and, conceivably, to lower unit costs.

For many of the above reasons, the British experience should be analyzed in detail as a possible precursor of some of the pressures which the United States may experience if it enters into a period of substantially reduced military spending. In particular, British efforts to channel effectively military technology into civil uses should be carefully watched, particularly if the Maddock recommendations are implemented.

Notes

1. This section borrows from Suomela *et al.*, pp. 94–124; and Franko, pp. 10, 21–22, and 32–34.

2. Wyn Grant, *The Political Economy of Industrial Policy* (London: Butterworths, 1982), p. 54; and Michael Davenport, "Industrial Policy in the United Kingdom" in F. G. Adams and L. R. Klein, *Industrial Policies for Growth and Competitiveness* (Lexington, Massachusetts: D.C. Heath, 1983), p. 342.

3. It is interesting to note, however, that two industries, aerospace and electical engineering received the larger part of R&D assistance, with 50% and 19% respectively in 1980.

4. N.K. Gardner, "Economics of Launching Aid" in Alan Whiting (ed.), *The Economics of Industrial Subsidies* (London: HMSO, 1976), p. 145.

5. Organization for European Cooperation and Development, *The Export Credit Financing System* (Paris: OECD, 1982), p. 229.

6. British Technology Group Press Briefing, 9 November 1984.

7. See "Britain's Ivory Tower Goes High Tech," *Science*, March 29, 1985, pp. 1560–1562.

8. The case of the steel industry is well-outlined in E. Cottrell, *The Giant With Feet of Clay* (London: Centre for Policy Studies, 1981).

9. The SFI program was begun in May 1982 to group together aid formerly available separately through the Research Requirements Boards or under the old Product and Process Development Scheme. It has focused on microelectronics, biotechnology, fibre-optics, and advanced manufacturing technology.

10. The European Community and its member states initiated at almost the same time a remarkably similar program known as the European Strategic Program for Research and Development in Information Technologies (ESPRIT). ESPRIT research and development will cover advanced microelectronics, software technology, advanced information processing, office automation, and computer-integrated manufacturing. The European Commission will contribute 50% and occasionally more to the cost of individual research projects. The Commission atrributes the disappointing level of accomplishment of European industry to inadequate cross-frontier business and research collaboration among member states, inadequate venture capital to create small and medium-sized high technology firms, duplication of national research efforts, nontariff barriers to intra-EEC trade, and public procurement preferences for domestic firms by member governments. The first five year phase of ESPRIT covering 1984–1988 is estimated to cost about $1.3 billion, of which $650 million will be paid directly by the Commission. ESPRIT projects are designed to aid only in the R&D phase of the effort to improve information technology in order to avoid commercial rivalry among participants.

11. See "Military Hardware Demand Boosts Cooperative Programs in Europe," *Aviation Week and Space Technology*, March 10, 1986, pp. 79–83, especially p. 81.

12. See "Airbus Industrie Officials Confident on Obtaining Funding for A330/A340," *Aviation Week and Space Technology*, June 16, 1986, p. 49.

13. See "German Airbus Partner Warns of Possible Finance Problems," *Aviation Week and Space Technology*, December 15, 1986, p. 33.

14. This section is based, in part, on Yuill & Allen, *European Regional Incentives, 1984*, pp. 52–54, and 373–423, and on updated information provided by the Department of Trade and Industry.

15. This document drew heavily from a study of the Department of Trade and Industry, *Regional Industrial Policy: Some Economic Issues*, (London: DTI, 1984).

16. Yuill and Allen, *European Regional Incentives, 1984*, p. 54.

17. See "British Select Boeing AWACS, Cancel Nimrod AEW Program," *Aviation Week and Space Technology*, December 22, 1986, p. 22; "Britain Picks Boeing's Plane over Nimrod," *Wall Street Journal*, December 9, 1986, p. 27; "From Nimrod to AWACS," *The Economist*, December 20, 1986, pp. 14–15; "Nimrod's Woes Are Latest GEC Setback," and "Nimrod Lasted Despite Problems, Say the US Proponents of AWACS," *Wall Street Journal*, December 18, 1986, p. 28; "Wide Attacks on Thatcher Expected in Debate Over US, UK Radar Planes," *Wall Street Journal*, December 16, 1986, p. 38; and "Mrs. Thatcher Faces No-Win Situation Picking US or British Airborne Radar," *Wall Street Journal*, December 12, 1986, p. 30.

18. On the other hand a firm "loses several degrees of freedom" in partnership. Added constraints appear in determining the optumum manfacturing pattern for an engine, in the "make or buy" decision, subcontracting, etc. For a variety of reasons, collaboration with "equals" tends to be more successful, but this is not always possible.

19. See "Britain Increases Science Spending," *Science,* December 6, 1985, pp. 1144–1145.

20. Sir Ieuan Maddock, "Commercial Exploitation of Defense Technology." Report to the National Economic Development Office, EDC/ELEC (82) 25, 14 September 1982, p. 15.

21. Maddock, "Commercial Exploitation of Defense Technology," p. 17.

22. See David Elliott and Hilary Wainwright, "The Lucas Plan: The roots of the Movement," in Suzanne Gordon and Dave McFadden (eds.), *Economic Conversion: Revitalizing America's Economy,* (Cambridge, MA: Ballinger Publishing Company, 1984), pp. 89–107.

23. Some promising recent work which examines some aspects of this issue is reviewed in Chapter 2 above.

Table 6.1 The United Kingdom: Number of Inventions
Submitted to NRDC, by Source, 1979/80 - 1982/83

SOURCE	1979-1980	1980-1981	1981-1982	1982-1983
GOVERNMENT RESEARCH DEPARTMENTS AND COUNCILS	421	491	555	580
HIGHER EDUCATION	413	505	532	590
PRIVATE INVENTORS	463	427	484	496
MISCELLANEOUS	61	45	27	38

Source: Department of Trade and Industry

7

Belgium

Industrial Policy[1]

Belgian industrial policy in the 1960s was directed at regional development and the improvement of the skills of its work force via investment grants, low interest loans, and tax breaks to many foreign firms in order to induce their establishment of subsidiaries in Belgium. In a drive to achieve scale economies and modernization, the government also encouraged the merger of domestic firms.

The program was quite successful and by the early 1970s one third of the country's industrial work force was employed in foreign-owned firms. When its own multinational firms were included, about half of employees in manufacturing were linked to production facilities abroad. The country's industrial structure took on typical multinational characteristics: high technology, high value added, high wages, and export orientation. In addition, trade unions played a major national role with a 70% unionization ratio, the highest in the industrial world.

During the 1973–1977 period, labor productivity in manufacturing increased rapidly. However, at the same time, the Belgian franc was rising in value which put substantial pressures on its traditional steel, clothing, and shipbuilding industries. The combination of higher productivity and competitive deterioration of traditional industries brought very high unemployment rates (over 11% in the first quarter of 1979).

At a time when other Western European countries were expelling their foreign "guest" workers, Belgium actually experienced a 10% increase in their number. It tried to sustain employment in steel and clothing by promoting EEC trade protection and crisis cartel measures. Small interest free loans were made available to firms preserving employment and limited nationalization and restructuring of the steel industry occurred. Increased tax relief measures, interest rate subsidies, accelerated depreciation, and large loan guarantees were added in 1978. Despite financial aid to electric authority buyers to encourage nuclear power and an expansion of aircraft parts production as part of the F-16 coproduction, public funding of R&D as a share of Gross Domestic Product fell slightly between 1974 and 1977.

In the early 1980s it was the government's intention to continue with the industrial development instruments then in place but with some shift from major funding to administrative assistance in seeking technology transfer opportunities, encouragement of exports to non-traditional markets, R&D coordination, selected government purchases, and increasing firm size. Despite some disputes with multinational firms they remain a favorite source for additional employment opportunities.

The situation was complicated by the passage of the Devolution Act of 1980 which formalized what had long been suspected; namely, that Belgium was actually three countries: Dutch speaking Flanders, French speaking Wallonia, and Brussels. The regions were given new authority and responsibilities but since the taxing authority remained federal the regions received no new resources to support these responsibilities.

The differential distribution of military industry between the regions leads to different strategies. Thus, Flanders essentially lacks a military industry which historically has been centered in Wallonia. Flanders therefore seeks militay contracts as leverage for future technological development while Wallonia uses R&D subsidies for civil programs to fill the gap in lost military production.

It is widely suspected that the national government's decision to begin production of a follow-on buy of 44 additional F-16's in 1984, rather than in 1986 as originally planned, was taken to assuage Walloon companies that lacked other orders to fill the gap. The Flemish Economic Union, a private employers organization, established FLAG (Flemish Aerospace Group) a couple of years ago as an industrial pressure group to get more compensation for military contracts. FLAG has its representatives in the cabinet of the President of the Flemish Government and, as such, the Flemish Government speaks on behalf of FLAG.

Very soon after its creation, FLAG not only asked for more compensation for Flemish companies but also for qualitatively higher compensation (high technological, high value added products). Today FLAG is particulary interested in spinoffs from military contracts because it would enable Flemish companies not only to become more independent of military contracts but it would also give them the basic technological knowledge to foster new high technology products.

This is perfectly illustrated by the compensation contract for the follow-on buy of 44 F-16s. Flanders demanded, and got, 52% compensation for this contract (about $120 million); all semi-direct and indirect compensation.

FLAG's philosophy is that direct compensation can be more interesting from the technological point of view in the short run, but, in the long run, it offers no follow-on contracts. Semi-direct and indirect compensation, however, although far more difficult to negotiate, is generating other nonmilitary contracts for the future.

The Walloon Regional Government and the industry's representatives are in a more difficult position. The Walloon companies operating in the military field are highly specialized in the production of military goods (e.g., F.N.,

SABCA, SONACA, PRB). Therefore, the Walloon Government typically negotiates direct compensation in military contracts. It tries to stretch these contracts into the future by negotiating as part of compensation a percentage of the parent company's sales to third parties, as in the F-16 Memorandum of Understanding.

The Walloon industrial lobby has attempted to get additional aid from national sources. The Walloon Minister who is responsible for science policy has set up a special aeronautical fund of about BF 10 billion ($167 million) spread over several years to help the national aeronautical industry in its R&D efforts. FN in 1984 got some BF 300–400 million so that it could participate in the PW-4000 civil engine program after a sharp fall in its assembly of Pratt and Whitney F-100 engines and SONACA in the same year got BF 1600 million for its participation in the A320 program.

The Flemish Government apparently refused official participation in this special aeronautical fund because it demands regional authority over subsidies to the industry. It does not accept that a French speaking national minister has authority over a national fund for this purpose. Like so many Belgian issues, it is very difficult to untangle the economic from the political strands.

Regional Policy[2]

The Belgian regional incentive package consists of an interest subsidy, a capital grant alternative to the subsidy, an accelerated depreciation allowance, several minor tax advantages and progress contracts toward an agreed development program. Labor training aids are biased in favor of problem areas via more beneficial award rates.

The interest subsidy is a discretionary project-related concession on interest payments on loans by approved credit institutions. The capital grant is also discretionary and project-related.

As a result of the devolution developments mentioned above, there have been changes in the administration of Belgian regional policy and basic decision making power. They are now located at the regional level.[3] New designated areas have been added and they now cover almost 35% of the national population. However, this represents a decline from the 39.5% under the previous Development Zones structure.

Military Industry Experiences

The major Belgian aerospace firm SABCA is heavily dependent on military sales. It has recently been as high as 95% and was expected to reach 70% in 1985 after subtracting the 10% accounted for by space activities. The company is attempting to increase its civil market share and in addition to the work on the A310 and A320 Airbus models is trying to develop a joint venture with an American partner on a new agricultural aircraft.

Since 1980, military procurement has declined some—essentially due to the high value of the dollar and the high cost of fuel. These forces resulted in reduced procurement and maintenance outlays by the Belgian Air Force.

The principal forms of adjustment aid as noted earlier consist of supporting firms to maintain their activities in economically depressed regions and assisting R&D activities leading to new product lines. A SABCA executive doubted the effectiveness of the first because of its support for passive attitudes on the part of the firms involved. However, he considered the second as promising since it stimulates private-initiatives and helps small companies.

Notes

1. This section borrows from Franko, *European Industrial Policy: Past, Present, and Future,* pp. 16, 37–40 and 58. The economic counselor and his staff at the US Embassy in Brussels were also particularly helpful.

2. This section is based on Yuill and Allen, *European Regional Incentives,* 1984, pp. 43, 119–143.

3. Responsibility for industry was shifted to the new regions but five problem industries already receiving subsidies were retained as a national responsibility. These were steel, glassmaking, textiles, coal, and shipbuilding. The first two were heavily concentrated in Wallonia. Of interest is the approach taken by the Walloon executive. Four objectives were established:

- to require private sector participation assuming at least 20% of the expense of any financially supported industrial research project;
- to concentrate on a limited number of areas in which promising developments had already been made in Wallonia, such as biotechnology, robotics, and use of new materials;
- to encourage foreign firms and researchers to form joint ventures in Wallonia;
- to provide venture capital to aid the launching of new firms or new projects by existing firms.

See "It's Hard Going: A Survey of Belgium," *The Economist,* February 22, 1986, p. 15. This excellent survey of economic and political developments in Belgium takes a hopeful attitude toward the country's ability to overcome recent economic difficulties and to escape its history of linguistic turmoil. How difficult this latter task will be was illustrated in late 1986 by yet another linguistic dispute. See "Le Belge Est Toujours Ridicule," *The Economist,* October 18, 1986, p. 51.

8

The Netherlands

Industrial Policy[1]

Industrial policy in the Netherlands paralleled that of Belgium in promoting industry, regional development and foreign investment through a package of grants, fiscal incentives, government loan guarantees, and the attraction of cheap natural gas for energy intensive industries. Its restructuring of the state-owned DSM (Dutch State Mines) from a coal company into a chemical products company was a great success.

The Netherlands was unique among Western European states in entering the mid-1970s crisis with no significant energy inhibition. Its reserves of natural gas gave it the lowest degree of dependence on imported energy in Europe. However, the rapid appreciation of the guilder in the mid-1970s reflected, in part, the decision to develop rapidly the production and export of gas. This exposed Dutch industry to competitive challenges similar to those encountered by its less well-endowed neighbors. In the presence of a strong currency and steadily increasing social costs, Dutch industry had to increase labor productivity at a rapid rate to compete on international markets. Unemployment rates, which increased about two percentage points between 1973 and 1978, were held down by a nearly one third reduction in the number of foreign workers. This process was particularly rapid in the clothing industry, where employment fell by almost 40% in the 1973–1977 period.

Its own energy resources could not cushion the blow which the world energy situation imposed on the Dutch shipbuilding sector. While productivity increases in capital intensive industries like chemicals kept pace they were not rapid enough to prevent the disappearance of many small firms in the clothing industry.

The Netherlands' free market tradition predisposed the nation to accept the disappearance of whole industries with less resistance than its neighbors. These free market traditions meant that Dutch industry was largely on its own in adjusting to the difficult economic situation in the 1974–77 period. Public attempts to help were initially general, and largely independent of any sectoral policy. Initially they took the form of expanding the tax allowances and investment grants offered to firms investing in the less developed northern and southern areas of the country. Several government-owned regional investment finance companies were also established, and increased subsidies were given to firms and individual workers to promote labor mobility and retraining.

As the recession worsened, however, the policy changed. Technology policy, as well as employment concerns, underlay decisions to provide large state loan guarantees to the hard-hit Fokker-VFW aircraft and Volvo-Daf car firms. The latter also received equity support from the state. The dramatic near disappearance of the Dutch clothing industry prompted Dutch approval of the EEC's tightening of the Multifiber Agreement. State subsidized loans or guarantees to the shipbuilding industry, and to its suppliers became frequent.

By 1976 almost by inadvertence, the Netherlands was providing subsidies to enterprises (exclusive of tax breaks or investment grants) equal to almost 3% of its GDP. Public funding for civilian R&D approached 0.9% of GDP, most of which went to public and university activities rather than to the support of commercial innovation.

In 1977, restructuring programs were introduced for the rapidly contracting shipbuilding and textile sectors, as well as for metal working. Although formal tripartite (labor, management, government) consultation normally occurred only on a national advisory level, a tripartite Restructuring Board (NEHEM) was set up by the Ministry of Economics to oversee the orderly contraction of these industries.

In 1977, a greatly increased program of tax credit, loan, and cash grant incentives to investment, was also proposed (the Investment Account Law). This program applied across all industry. Because of its nonselectivity and scope, the EEC Commission objected to the Law. The Netherlands was forced to reduce the scale and increase the selectivity of its program. The EEC also obliged the Netherlands to rescind those portions of the Investment Account Law which would have given regional premiums to investments undertaken in well over half of the country, as well as premiums to help pay for purely replacement investments. The law was passed in modified form in 1978.

Despite a better than average economic performance, the Netherlands appears increasingly concerned with its industrial competitive position and a move towards promotion of industry is under way. However, there has been some negative reaction to the rapid increase in public funds going almost exclusively to firms in economic distress.

The modified version of the Investment Account Law of May 1978 is designed to promote new industrial investment through general, regional, and small business investment premiums. Large income tax rebates and cash grants are planned into the 1980s. Modest increases in government funding will be provided for research and development, especially for the development and use of energy saving and environmental protection technologies.

The government also is promoting the restructuring of industry, which will see a move away from declining sectors. Subsidies will be publicized so tax-payers will know more about their nature and cost. More emphasis is planned on attaining the business-labor-government social consensus through the Restructuring Board (NEHEM).

Export promotion is also being emphasized with subsidies and guarantees for the preparation of bids on major turnkey projects.

Regional Policy[2]

The two main incentives in the Dutch regional aid bundle have been the investment premium (Investeringspremieregeling, IPR), and the regional component of the investment account scheme (Wet Investeringsrekening, WIR).

The investment premium is the key Dutch regional aid. It is a project-related capital grant, and is administered in an essentially automatic way for projects with eligible investment of up to 18 million florins (Fl). For larger projects, only the award of the first Fl 18 million of eligible investment is automatic. In effect, any award going beyond that amount is wholly discretionary.

The WIR regional and physical planning are to be abolished under a bill finally passed in May 1984. This was a complex situation and it involved disputes with the EEC and among the Dutch political parties. It is generally agreed that the WIR allowances were not very effective despite their considerable cost and they will not be discussed further here.

The Dutch system of regional incentives has been substantially reduced and by July 1985 less than a fourth of the population were living in designated problem areas.

Military Firm Experiences

Two Dutch producers of military equipment were contacted and both responded: Philips International B.V., the large multinational electronics firm; and Fokker, B.V., the aerospace firm.

Philips has defense companies in the NATO countries (including the United States), and in Sweden. All of them produce both military and civil products and the military share ranges from 10 to 90%. Overall, defense sales account for around 5 to 6% of total corporate sales. While the Dutch government has encouraged firms not to become "too" dependent on defense contracts its policy has been to bring the greatest possible benefit, both directly and indirectly, to the economy.

At Fokker, the level of dependence on military sales is about one fifth, with a slight decrease in prospect as the F-16 production declines. The current ten year defense plan through 1994 does not show an overall decrease in military spending. However the composition will change with more going to aircraft armaments, ground and ship-based missile systems, tanks, helicopters, and substantial modifications to update the F-16. The company foresees a continuing good military market.

On the civil side, Fokker has launched two new programs; the Fokker 50 replacement for the workhorse F-27 and the Fokker 100, the successor to the F-28. Early responses have been very favorable and the company sees the F-100 as a likely purchase for many major airlines. It is of interest to note that these two new aircraft were developed in response to the market and not due to a reduction in military spending.

While there are government policies to aid firms facing economic difficulties, they have been used most visibly in suport of the shipbuilding industry which has been hurt by competition from companies in Southeast Asia. While a major Dutch shipbuilder was allowed to go bankrupt in 1984 it was unrelated to reduced military spending.

Notes

1. This section borrows from Franko, *European Industrial Policy: Past, Present, and Future*, pp. 16, 40–42, and 59–60.

2. This section is based on Yuill and Allen, *European Regional Incentives*, 1984, pp. 50–52, and 347–372.

9

Italy

Industrial Policy[1]

On the basis of ownership of the means of production, ownership of the channels of finance, and the provision of public services, the government of Italy is more involved in industry than any other Western European government. Yet, Italian officials repeatedly assert that Italy has little or no industrial policy if this be taken to mean consistently promoting, protecting, or shrinking particular sectors as is done in France, Germany, or Britain.

Italy has had an extensive regional policy. Since the 1950s, Italy has promoted private investment in the South through investment grants, low interest loans and tax breaks, and has required state owned companies to invest in the South. The regional priority in industrial investment was strengthened. In the mid-1970s, this reflected a growing political consensus that the social cost to the cities of the North of massive in-migrations of labor during the 1950s and 1960s had been too high.

Italy also had a tradition of using state-owned industries, banks, and services to serve the macro-economic goal of maintaining aggregate investment activity during recessions. This policy dates back to the Great Depression, when the Institute of Industrial Reconstruction (IRI) was founded to take over and revive a wide range of failing companies.

The most notable addition to state industrial institutions during the 1970s was the Gestione e Partecipazione Industriale (GEPI), a financial holding and management consulting company specifically charged with a salvage mission in 1971 after the recession of 1969–1970. Italian policy during the mid-1970s largely expanded the regional, countercyclical, and employment maintenance orientations of previous policies toward industry. Salvage (or "breathing space") loans to state companies to continue their investment programs, and to private companies to enable them to keep operating and to invest more in the South became widespread. Public financing of industrial investment has probably reached a higher proportion of total investment than anywhere else in Europe. Medium-term public financing went to support both current operations and investments of troubled companies in the machine tool, chemical, steel, shipbuilding, auto, and aircraft industries. New or expanded state ownership occurred in the textile industry. New

state equity capital was also injected into such state
Romeo.

Italy's mid 1970s policies toward industry were muc
particular sectors than were the industrial policies of Frar
While Italy supported individual companies in trouble, it
them in the North. Indeed, the activities of the salvage ag
limited to the South only. Britain, on the other hand, res   ..panies
of all types nearly everywhere through a combination of regional aids and
employment subsidies. Also, due in part to the fragmentation of Italian
industry, suporting a troubled company rarely involved intervention in an
entire industry. Italian industry historically has been much less concentrated
in large company groups than that of the UK, and it includes many successful
small and medium-sized firms.

Finsider, the state steel company, suffered from many of the financial
problems of its British and French counterparts, and sought some of the
same remedies. However, Finsider's financial troubles reflected socially
imposed retention of excessive numbers of employees, rather than the
technological obsolescence characteristic of many British and French plants.

State takeovers and subsidies provided respite for a few Italian textile
and clothing firms. Italian firms in this industry received protection from
extra-EEC competitors as a result of the 1977 tightening of the Multifiber
Agreement. Taken as a whole however, the Italian clothing industry was
quite successful. While the clothing industries of other European countries
rapidly declined, employment in the Italian clothing industry declined little,
and its trade balance became increasingly positive.

Despite the intervention tool kit at the disposal of the Italian government,
some argue that Italy is one of the more laissez-faire economies in the
West. State supported funding of civilian R&D is far below levels in other
industralized countries. Small and medium-sized enterprises constitute a
larger share of the economy than in most other countries.

There are some fears that large state programs will lead to unfair
competition with private companies. There is talk of a limit to further state
company acquisitions to protect the dynamism of private industry, especially
of the many highly successful small and medium-sized firms in Italy. This
is reflected in the stated aim of the GEPI "rescue" organization to return
firms to the private sector once their commercial viability has been rees-
tablished.

Italian unions, although traditionally more class-conscious and unyielding
in wage bargaining are generally considered to have behaved in a way
conducive to efficiency and productivity increases.

There appears to have been a consensus among the main political forces
that the strength of the Italian economy was due in part to the dynamism
of smaller enterprises and that aid to larger firms, especially large state
owned firms, should be minimized.

Italian industrial policy has remained regional rather than reactive; rescue-
oriented and firm-specific rather than directed toward whole industries.

.iile the private enterprise sector is still being allowed to go its own ay, Italy has developed a comprehensive plan for the state enterprise sector.

Paradoxically, as a result of a tradition of lax enforcement of tax and social security laws on smaller firms, entrepreneurship is rewarded to a much greater degree than in most other Western nations. Few countries have been less restrictive of multinational corporate operations.

Regional Policy[2]

There are four principal types of incentives available in the Italian Mezzogiorno or South: a grant awarded by the Cassa per il Mezzogiorno; a loan/interest subsidy funded in part by the so-called "National Fund for Subsidized Credit"; a concession on social security contributions paid by employers to INPS (the main social security institute in Italy); and three tax concessions, two relating to the local income tax, ILOR (imposta locale sui redditi), and one to the profits tax, IRPEG (imposta sui reddito delle persone-giuridiche). Beyond these incentives, there are a number of smaller "national" regional aids, as well as some incentives awarded by the autonomous regions. Among these more minor aids are the incentives awarded by the autonomous regions. These include the Mediocredito soft loan scheme for small and medium-sized firms, an interest subsidy for groups (consorzi) of problem-area authorities, the provision of equity finance, and concessions on electricity bills for very small firms. None of these minor incentives is, however, of any significance within the Mezzogiorno and indeed few have been awarded in the South in recent years.

Taking the main incentives in turn, the Cassa grant is an automatic, project-related capital grant with a basic rate of award ranging from 40% for smaller projects to just over 20% for the largest projects. Projects in priority sectors *or* priority areas receive one fifth above the basic grant while projects in priority sectors *and* areas receive two-fifths above the basic grant, giving a maximum award of 56%. The 'National Fund' scheme is a national project-related scheme but both eligibility conditions and rates of award favor the Mezzogiorno. In the Mezzogiorno, the rate of interest charged is 64% below the average market rate for medium and long-term loans, the loan principal covers 40% of global investment and the loan duration is of between 10 and 15 years with a 3–5 year principal repayment holiday— making it the most valuable regional interest-related subsidy in the European Community.

The social security concession is a full (100%) concession on employee social security contributions to INPS for labor hired after 1 July 1976 where that labor represents an addition to the establishment's work force (as at 30 June 1976). The concession is automatic, is limited to the Mezzogiorno and is payable for 10 years from the date the additional labor is hired. Finally, the three tax concessions are: a ten-year ILOR exemption for industrial projects in the Mezzogiorno and small industrial projects in parts of the Center-North; an exemption on up to 70% of the ILOR Tax liability where taxable profits are used to invest in the Mezzogiorno; and a ten-year exemption on 50% of IRPEG for firms which are founded and locate their headquarters in the Mezzogiorno.

A number of points should be made about the Mezzogiorno package. First, it is a wide-ranging package, covering all the main regional incentive types and including, too, the only major labor-related subsidy in the Community. Second, it is one of the most valuable packages in the Community. However, this maximum is restricted to relatively small projects (reflecting the strong emphasis in Italy on the promotion of small and medium-sized firms) and declines fairly rapidly as project size increases. A further feature of the Mezzogiorno package is its basically automatic administrative system. No other regional incentive scheme in the Community has the virtually complete absence of administrative discretion that is found among the main Mezzogiorno aids. Finally, the future of the Cassa per il Mezzogiorno and related Mezzogiorno policies is unclear at present.[3] The current law has only remained in force since 1980 by virtue of a series of decrees and extensions passed by ministerial ruling.

Experience of Military Producers

The experience of two Italian firms will be reported: Elettronica, a specialist in electronic warfare systems, and Aeritalia, the major Italian aerospace firm.

Elettronica is almost completely dependent on military sales. A token 1% represents a line of new products which developed as a fallout of research originally aimed at military applications and later applied to complex biomedical equipment and automated devices.

For Aeritalia, defense production accounts for only 40% of the total. Commercial aircraft work has grown steadily in recent years. This reflects cooperative agreements with Boeing in the 767, with McDonnell-Douglas for the production of major assemblies for the DC-10 and MD-80, and with Aerospatiale of France in a 50-50 venture calling for the design and production of the ATR 42, a twin turboprop regional commuter aircraft. As air traffic grows the corresponding increase in the demand for new aircraft should help Aeritalia's civil market development. In addition, the company has broadened its scope of operations by taking an interest in Selenia, a weapon and electronics system developer[4], and by acquiring the aeroengine facilities of Alfa Romeo Aviazione. These include overhaul, production of critical components, and R&D. It is estimated that at least half of these facilities will be engaged in civil market activities. Aeritalia's subsidiary company Partenavia, focuses on general (private) aviation which should grow with improved economic conditions.

Elettronica's work in biomedical equipment and automated devices is expected to grow moderately and other types of civil oriented products are also under consideration by the company. In the foreseeable future, however, electronic warfare is likely to remain the principal activity.

The Italian government has made no statements on possible reductions in military procurement and informed persons dismiss the idea of such reductions as unlikely. If a concern exists, it deals with export markets which are seen as essential to the survival of the European defense industry since domestic requirements would neither support nor justify production in economical volumes and even less, R&D costs. No shortage of NATO military orders is anticipated and much modernization is seen in prospect.

Italian defense firm executives are unaware of specific aids to firms facing difficulties due to reductions in defense procurement. Such problems would be addressed by more general programs.

Notes

1. Franko, *European Industrial Policy: Past, Present, and Future*, pp. 35–37, and 59.

2. This section is based on Yuill and Allen, *European Regional Incentives*, 1984, pp. 283–284.

3. At last report the Cassa was to be replaced by a National Fund for the Development of the Mezzogiorno (Fondo Nazionale per lo Sviluppo del Mezzogiorno) in which the regions will assume a greater role in implementing development programs. For recent views on the Mezzogiorno problem, see "North-South: Italy—The Mending of the Mezzogiorno," *The Economist*, August 15, 1986, pp. 30–31; and "Italy's Mezzogiorno is a Social Time Bomb," *Wall Street Journal*, December 12, 1986, p. 30.

4. Selenia is trying to reduce its present relatively high dependence on military work (75%) and established an office in Washington in early 1986. Its goal is to increase collaborative work with the US government and private industry in areas relevant to the Strategic Defense Initiative and air traffic control systems. See "Selenia Aims at Expanded Share of US Defense, ATC Contracts," *Aviation Week and Space Technology*, February 24, 1986, pp. 89–91.

10

Conclusions

The findings of this study suggest that changing levels and changing compositions of military spending present challenges to firms, communities, and individuals which are not different essentially from other forms of market change which occur in a dynamic economy.

Programs designed to encourage firms and sectors to expand their markets were found throughout Western Europe. These range from beneficial access to capital for R&D and production through export guarantees and encouragement of multi-national collaborative ventures. This is particularly true for firms and sectors viewed as crucial to national security and well being. Unless the government provides a market by its own public procurement activities, however, success or failure of the effort to diversify markets will largely be determined by the ability of company management to locate a market whose needs it can meet at a competitive price.

Thus, the enhancement of technological capabilities which has been much emphasized is only part of the story. "Market pull" is likely to be more important than "technology push" in successful operation in civil markets. Some suspect that the reverse condition prevails in military markets; that is, that technological capabilities take precedence over price when selling to the military. If this is true, a successful transition may require organizational structures based on separate divisions which would permit segregation between military and civilian markets. Under such circumstances, separate design, production, and marketing would be emphasized to tailor products to their respective markets. In this regard, it will be interesting to trace the results of the Saab-Scania reorganization in Sweden.

Finally, the overall societal attitude to change is also a significant determinant of the outcome of the transition challenge. A society wedded to particular organizational forms and operating procedures will likely face a more difficult transitional experience. This suggests that policies in aid of a successful transition might better focus on broad environmental issues and attitudes and less on the day-to-day experiences of particular firms and sectors. The risks of over-protection and subsequent loss of vitality are real.

On the other hand, short-term transitional assistance to displaced workers, firms, and communities suffering from sharply reduced or redirected defense spending would appear to be both effective and fair. Such assistance measures would be most useful if they provide for retraining and relocation of workers rather than simply help fund a form of "wait" unemployment or encourage inventory accumulation of products whose markets are disappearing. Some of the policies in place in Western Europe which have been reviewed above have interesting characteristics which usefully could be studied by American policymakers concerned with the adjustment problem.

Index